The Gossamer Years

*

*

*

The *Gossamer Years*

(*Kagerō Nikki*)

*

The Diary of
a Noblewoman
of
Heian Japan

Translated by
Edward Seidensticker

Tokyo, Japan &
Rutland, Vermont

CHARLES E. TUTTLE COMPANY: PUBLISHERS

UNESCO COLLECTION OF REPRESENTATIVE WORKS
JAPANESE SERIES
This book has been accepted in the Japanese Series
of the Translations Collection
of the United Nations Educational,
Scientific and Cultural Organization (UNESCO)

Representatives

For Continental Europe:
BOXERBOOKS, INC., *Zurich*

For the British Isles:
PRENTICE-HALL INTERNATIONAL, INC., *London*

For Australasia:
BOOK WISE (AUSTRALIA) PTY. LTD.
104-108 Sussex Street, Sydney 2000

Published by the Charles E. Tuttle Company, Inc.
of Rutland, Vermont & Tokyo, Japan
with editorial offices at Suido 1-chome, 2-6, Bunkyo-ku, Tokyo

Copyright in Japan, 1964 by Charles E. Tuttle Company, Inc.

Library of Congress Catalog Card No. 64-22750

International Standard Book No. 0-8048-1123-7

First edition, 1964
First Tut Book edition, 1973
Fourth printing, 1981

0295-000142-4615
PRINTED IN JAPAN

Contents

Introduction *page 7*

The Gossamer Years *page 31*
Book One
Book Two
Book Three

Notes *page 169*

Appendix:
The Heian Setting: Illustrations and Map
page 203

Introduction

AN EARLIER version of this translation was finished in 1952 and published by the Asiatic Society of Japan in 1955. Shortly afterwards there was talk of republication by UNESCO, but the translation was thought by the potential sponsor to be excessively free. In the end he suggested that it be revised.

Feeling myself that the opening sentences in particular were a bit free, I undertook the revision, which was completed in 1960 and is offered herewith. Certain thoughts which came to me in the process of retranslation are appended to this introduction. They are reprinted, with slight revisions, from the *Japan Quarterly* of October-December 1960 (VII: 4). The reader who compares the revision with the earlier translation will find that changes are to be explained in three ways: by mistakes in that translation; by advances in textual criticism and particularly the appearance of the Iwanami edition in late 1957; and by a shift toward literalness in the principles governing the translation.

*

Though it will be referred to as a diary, the *Kagerō Nikki* is in fact a combined autobiography-diary covering twenty-one years in the life of a mid-Heian Fujiwara noblewoman known today as "the mother of Michitsuna." It is the record of her unhappy marriage to her kinsman, Fujiwara Kaneie, beginning in 954 with his first love letters, and ending in 974 with their very nearly complete estrangement. In the intervening years the author has occasion to record her indignation at successive revelations of rival wives and mistresses (Kaneie had some eight or nine of whom a record remains), and the diary is in a sense her protest against the marriage system of the time, and her exposition of the thesis that men are beasts.

Traditionally there have been two theories of the meaning of *kagerō*: either it is a sort of mayfly, or it is one of those shimmerings of the summer sky which, for want of a more poetic term, we call a "heat wave." Recently a third theory has been advanced. Professor Kawaguchi Hisao, the editor of the new Iwanami text, argues that *kagerō* means gossamer in the original sense, defined thus by Webster: "A film of cobwebs floating in the air in calm, clear weather." Little evidence is presented in support of the theory, however, and one may suspect that it derives from Dr. Arthur Waley, who has called the work *The Gossamer Diary*. Dr. Waley's lead has of course been followed in naming this retranslation. His title makes up in poetic worth for what it lacks in philological.

The expression *kagerō no nikki* (or, in common usage, *kagerō nikki*) is to be found in a passage at the end of Book I in which the author looks back over her life and comments on the insubstantiality of things. "Indeed, as I think of the unsatisfying events I have recorded here, I wonder whether I have been describing anything of substance. Call it, this journal of mine, a shimmering of the summer sky."

The first part of the work is not a true diary but a brief set of memoirs written considerably after the facts treated. Gradually, however, the incidents become more detailed, and the last half of Book 2 and all of Book 3 seem more like day-to-day journal notations. Book 1, the shortest of the three, covers fifteen years, while Books 2 and 3, of approximately equal length, cover only three years each. The year 971 receives the most detailed attention of all, and from the tone of the narrative one may guess that the work was begun in that year, possibly when, as recorded toward the end of Book 2, the author returned to the city from a mountain temple and began to lose interest in Kaneie and his new affairs. Perhaps she gathered herself for an appraisal of her life and an effort to record her version of the long struggle. Book 3 is somewhat different from the other two, quieter and more restrained, and the diary breaks off with the author apparently reconciled to a lonely and uneventful middle age on the outskirts of the city.

Very little is known of the author and her life aside from the incidents recorded in the diary. She was born to the provincial-governor class, the second stratum in the Fujiwara clan hierarchy, and thus a level below her husband, who was the nephew of the Regent[1] and who himself subsequently succeeded to that office. The provincial-governor class, though generally treated with mild contempt in Heian literature, was the class that produced the great Heian women authors. The author of this diary was an aunt of the author of the *Sarashina Nikki* (Sarashina Diary). One of her sisters was married to a great-uncle of Murasaki Shikibu, author of the *Genji Monogatari* (Tale of Genji), and one of her brothers was married to a sister of Sei Shōnagon, author of the *Makura no Sōshi* (The Pillow Book).

The author's father, Fujiwara Tomoyasu, held minor posts in the capital until after her marriage, and it is therefore fairly certain that she spent her youth in Kyoto. Her name and the date of her birth are not known.

For someone in her class to be taken even as the second wife of such a well-placed young gentleman as Kaneie would have been considered a fine stroke of luck by most Heian ladies. But the author of the *Kagerō Nikki,* the genealogical tables[2] tell us, was one of the three outstanding beauties of her day. She was too impetuous to be satisfied with her position as a subsidiary wife. She wanted a husband of her own, she informs us, ''thirty days and thirty nights a month,'' and each of Kaneie's promotions meant only that she saw less of him. Her resentment against Kaneie and her venomous rage at her rivals form the base and many of the high points of the diary.

Almost nothing is known of the author's life after 974. A collection of poems appended to the diary (and to the 1955 version of this translation) indicates that she was still active as a poet in 993. She died at the latest in 995, perhaps in the

---

[1] Who wielded power in the Emperor's name. *Sesshō* when the Emperor was a child; otherwise *Kampaku.*

[2] *Sompi Bummyaku,* first compiled in the fourteenth century.

smallpox epidemic of that year. An entry in the *Shōyūki,* the diary of Kaneie's cousin Sanesuke, describes a memorial rite held in 996 on the anniversary of her death, but does not specify which anniversary. Kaneie continued to look for new lady friends until his death in 990.

The accompanying tables, compiled from *Sompi Bummyaku, Dainihon Jimmei Jisho,* and *Kagerō Nikki no Kōgi* (for the last, see below) indicate family ties among the principal figures in the diary.

The *Kagerō Nikki* was known in the late Heian and Kamakura periods, and is mentioned in the early Kamakura journal of Fujiwara Teika. The oldest surviving texts, however, date from the seventeenth century. The first textual study was the annotation by the Priest Keichū, a seventeenth-century student of the Japanese classics, of what he called "the Mito book." It survives in the Shōkōkan, the library of the Mito Tokugawa family. Three dated wood-block editions appeared during the Tokugawa period, the first two identical (apparently the same blocks were used) and the third with but minor variations. It is not known what manuscript they were taken from. There is also an undated edition. The principal Tokugawa commentary is the *Kagerō Nikki Kaikan* (1775), the work of a scholar who used the pen name Han Chō. It is far from reliable.

There are two important modern commentaries, both of which render the text into modern Japanese: *A Course in the Kagerō Nikki* (Kagerō Nikki no Kōgi) by Kita Yoshio (Tokyo, Musashino Shoin, 1944) and *A New Commentary on the Kagerō Nikki* (Kagerō no Nikki Shinshaku) by Tsugita Jun and Onishi Zemmei (Tokyo, Meiji Shoin, 1960). The diary has also been put into modern Japanese by two important lady writers, the poetess Yosano Akiko and the novelist Enchi Fumiko; and the novelist Hori Tatsuo drew upon it freely for his *Kagerō no Nikki* (1939). Murō Saisei has made "the lady in the alley," one of Kaneie's more fleeting loves, the heroine of a novel. Of modern texts, the new Iwanami edition (edited by Kawaguchi Hisao, in *Nihon Koten Bungaku Taikei,* 1957) comes as near being definitive as anything is likely to be for some time. It is based on a Tokugawa-period

Table One

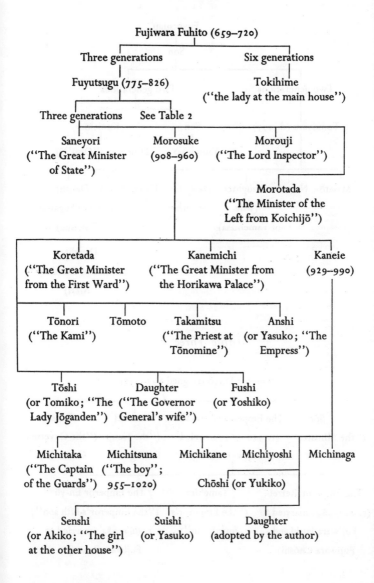

Fujiwara Fuhito (659–720)

Three generations — Six generations

Fuyutsugu (775–826) — Tokihime ("the lady at the main house")

Three generations — See Table 2

Saneyori ("The Great Minister of State") — Morosuke (908–960) — Morouji ("The Lord Inspector")

Morotada ("The Minister of the Left from Koichijō")

Koretada ("The Great Minister from the First Ward") — Kanemichi ("The Great Minister from the Horikawa Palace") — Kaneie (929–990)

Tōnori ("The Kami") — Tōmoto — Takamitsu ("The Priest at the Tōnomine") — Anshi (or Yasuko; "The Empress")

Tōshi (or Tomiko; "The Lady Jōganden") — Daughter ("The Governor General's wife") — Fushi (or Yoshiko)

Michitaka ("The Captain of the Guards") — Michitsuna ("The boy"; 955–1020) — Michikane — Michiyoshi — Michinaga

Chōshi (or Yukiko)

Senshi (or Akiko; "The girl at the other house") — Suishi (or Yasuko) — Daughter (adopted by the author)

Table Two

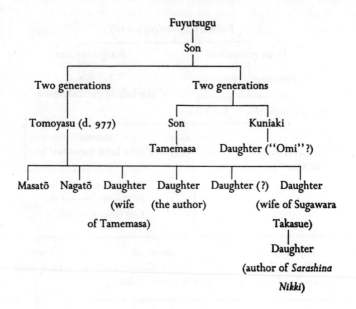

Fuyutsugu
Son

Two generations   Two generations

Tomoyasu (d. 977)   Son   Kuniaki

Tamemasa   Daughter ("Omi"?)

Masatō   Nagatō   Daughter   Daughter   Daughter (?)   Daughter
(wife   (the author)   (wife of Sugawara
of Tamemasa)   Takasue)

Daughter
(author of *Sarashina
Nikki*)

Table Three

The Emperor Daigo (reigned 897–930)

Son   The Emperor Murakami   Kaneaki   Takaaki
("the Minister")   (r. 946–967; married   ("the Genji   ("the Governor
to Fujiwara Anshi)   Dainagon")   General")

The Emperor Reizei   Tamehira   The Emperor En-yū
(r. 967–969; married to   ("the Emperor's   ("the Emperor's fifth son";
Fujiwara Fushi and   fourth son")   r. 969–984; married to
Fujiwara Chōshi)   Fujiwara Senshi)

text preserved in the Imperial Household Library (the Toshoryō). In revising the translation, I have followed the Iwanami text. Dr. Waley's partial translation appears in the introduction to the *Sacred Tree* volume of his *Genji* (London, Allen and Unwin, 1926). A complete translation into German has been made by Tsukakoshi Satoshi (Zurich, 1955).

✻

The *Kagerō Nikki* is a remarkably frank personal confession and a strong attempt to describe a difficult relationship and a disturbed state of mind. As such it occupies, I think, an extremely important place in the development of Heian literature. The essential fact of Heian prose literature at its best (and by its best one of course means the *Genji Monogatari*) is that it represents an extraordinary flowering of realistic expression, an attempt, unique for its age, to treat of the human condition with frankness and honesty.

It does not seem to me that the beginnings of this realism are to be found before the latter half of the tenth century. The *Tosa Nikki* (Tosa Diary) tells of an actual journey; but the events are such that it is really no more than an extravagant adventure story, a potpourri of storms and pirates and spells, designed to excite noble ladies who had never been beyond the city limits. The *Taketori Monogatari* (Tale of the Bamboo Cutter) shows the faint beginnings of character portrayal, but it is frankly a fairy story. For the rest, there are the *uta monogatari,* the "poem romances," collections of anecdotes built around poems of uneven value; and there are Buddhist parables.

With the *Ochikubo Monogatari* (Tale of the Basement Room) and the *Utsubo Monogatari* (Tale of the Hollow Tree) Japanese fiction for the first time descends to a concrete social situation. The *Ochikubo Monogatari* is concerned with the injustice of Heian marriage. In its comic scenes—the scene in which Michiyori and his attendant are knocked down in a well-manured street, for instance—it attains to a sort of Rabelaisian realism. But for the most part it deals with its social problem only indirectly: in effect, it runs away in search of an ideal world, and we can only infer from its treatment of the ideal what the nasty real world must have been like. Michiyori is a husband of unspeakable virtue, and the *Ochikubo Monogatari* does little to break the hold of the fairy tale on Japanese fiction. Much the same can be said of the *Utsubo Monogatari,* although in its later sections it does retreat from the undisguised fantasy with which it begins.

It is in this connection, I think, that the significance of the *Kagerō Nikki* becomes clear : it is the first attempt in Japanese literature, or in any case the first surviving attempt, to capture on paper, without evasion or idealization, the elements of a real social situation. The author sets down her purpose and declares her independence of her predecessors in the opening sentences of the diary. Referring to herself in the third person, she says: "... as the days went by in monotonous succession, she had occasion to look at the old romances, and found them masses of the rankest fabrication. Perhaps, she said to herself, even the story of her own dreary life, set down in a journal, might be of interest ; and it might also answer a question : had that life been one befitting a well-born lady?" Though now and then she reverts to the clumsiness of the *uta monogatari,* for the most part she holds bravely to that purpose.

There is evident, moreover, a steady growth in the author's narrative technique as the diary progresses. The hurried, fragmentary air of the earlier sections gives way in Book 3 to something very like realistic fiction. In particular the incidents surrounding Kaneie's brother Tōnori and the author's adopted daughter show a remarkable economy of detail and a skillful use of suspense and background. They cannot but have influenced Murasaki Shikibu if, as seems likely, she read them. They must have served at least to demonstrate the possibilities of a literature tied to plain reality.

Yet one cannot deny that the *Kagerō* lacks the imaginative breadth of the *Genji.* The author and her great problem are alone in a dark cave into which little light from the outside world enters. In a sense this isolation is characteristic of the society in which she lived : the Fujiwara were already losing their grip on the provinces, and the mid-tenth century saw two serious revolts ; but the courtiers were too busy with their parties and intrigues to pay much attention. The author of the *Kagerō Nikki* lived within still another shell within this shell. The intrigues seem to have interested her no more than the provincial disturbances interested the intriguers.

The period 967 to 972 was one of considerable political turmoil in Kyoto, but little suggestion of it reaches this diary. In 967 the Emperor Murakami died, after having made some slight attempt to hold out against the Fujiwara. Fujiwara Saneyori, the Minister of the Left, immediately became Regent. The only mention the author makes of this incident, of such importance to her family, is to note sardonically that there was a singular lack of gloom over the Emperor's death, and to send a poem of consolation to one of his concubines.

In 969 the Minister of the Left (Saneyori had meanwhile become Prime Minister), Minamoto Takaaki, was charged with plotting to have his son-in-law, Prince Tamehira, made crown prince, and was exiled to Kyushu. Had the plot succeeded (if indeed there was a plot) it would have been a serious threat to the power which the Fujiwara exercised through their imperial sons-in-law and grandsons. Although the growing truculence of the provincial warrior clans posed an unrecognized problem, Takaaki's exile put away the last immediate threat to Fujiwara supremacy for about a hundred years and ushered in the glittering and superficially prosperous period that reached a climax under the rule of Kaneie's son Michinaga. The incident receives fairly detailed treatment in the diary, but only because the author is thoroughly in sympathy with Takaaki. Either she is not aware of the threat his alleged scheming poses to her family, or else she is quite aware of it but sees a chance to snipe at the dominant Fujiwara clique and thus indirectly at her husband. Takaaki's return to Kyoto in 972 is not mentioned.

In 970 came the death of Saneyori and the succession of his nephew, Kaneie's brother Koretada, an event which in effect brought the Regency within Kaneie's reach, but which receives only the briefest mention in the diary. Then in 972, with Koretada's death, a fierce squabble broke out between Kaneie and his brother Kanemichi over the succession. The author notes at this point, with either an ignorance of or a disregard for the facts, that Kaneie "seemed to prosper." Kanemichi in fact won the battle, and Kaneie's career took a dip from which it did not begin to recover until Kanemichi's death in 977. It may be that the diary was written for ladies in waiting who did not need to be lectured to on political intrigue; but it seems more likely that, shut off with her problem, the author was but dimly aware of what was going on outside.

Hers, then, was a dark, narrow sort of realism. For the most part she was not able to see beyond herself. When in Book 3 she finally attained to something like a novelist's detachment, she evidently lost interest in her subject and stopped writing, and the imaginative jump to realistic fiction was left to her great successor a generation later. I do not think that much if any of the text is missing at the end of the diary. Book 3 breaks off, as did Books 1 and 2, on New Year's Eve. The evidence grows toward the end of Book 3 that the author has lost interest in the matter of her diary, the matter of her youth, and it seems not improbable that whoever came "pounding" that New Year's Eve distracted her from her writing, and that she saw no point in taking it up again.

It would be a mistake, I think, to conclude from the above that the diary is interesting only as a sort of preparatory document for something better to come. It has very real merit of its own, and now and then, particularly in Book 3, it seems to me to come almost up to the level of the *Tale of Genji*. All in all a very frank and appealing lady emerges from its pages, albeit a somewhat more spoiled and capricious one than she would have preferred us to see.

✳

Descriptions of the Heian period frequently emphasize its effeminacy and its moral corruption. It is true of course that life moved indoors, that the huntsman and the falconer gave way to the sampler of perfumes and the master calligrapher; and it is a source of some puzzlement to the Japanese that this first "pure Japanese" period in their history should have taken such an "un-Japanese" turn.

Perhaps the most striking feature of aristocratic Heian life, however, is its emphasis on good taste. Inaction, a word which seems to describe the tone of Heian life better than "effeminacy," gave rise to a vast and minute cultivation of taste and form. Infinite care was devoted to the selection of an ensemble, to the composition of a letter, to the concocting of a new perfume. While therefore the life of the Heian gentleman may seem a trifle dissolute to the puritan, it was never gross or vulgar. The number of love affairs he had did not matter, but the way in which he conducted them did. He fell in love with a young lady because he caught a glimpse of her unexceptionable sleeves, and he won her hand with slight little poems and a show of skill in calligraphy. Properly wan and melancholy as he moved from affair to affair, careful to follow all the rules of as elaborate a code as has ever been put together, he quite lacked the passionate rebelliousness of the true profligate.

Good taste was his religion, and he was not given to speculative thought. This is not to say that he had no use for revealed religion; rather that he was not much worried about putting the universe in order, that religious notions and ceremonies but served to intensify the sweet sad beauty of the moment, and that he found it not in the least uncomfortable to harbor a most incoherent mishmash of Shinto, Buddhism, Confucianism, necromancy, and witchcraft.

The most curious elements in this curious religious jumble derive ultimately from primitive Chinese divination. They have to do with activities prohibited or required by the necromancers. Certain days were bad for cutting the hair, other days were bad for sick calls, and one night in every sixty, the night of the *kōshin,* a person had to go sleepless lest certain dormant poisons seize an unguarded moment to do away with him. The movements of various gods carried with them taboos. Thus Taihakujin or Hitohimeguri moved to a different one of the eight directions every day, and it was forbidden to advance in the direction where he happened to be in residence. Two days in every ten were free, however, since he spent one day in the sky and one in the earth after completing a tour of the compass. Tenichijin or Nakagami stayed five or six days at each point, and his direction became taboo depending on the year of one's birth. Daishōgun stayed at each of the cardinal points for three years. Small errands were permitted, but major projects that might transgress upon his direction were forbidden. Konjin moved about by the year and carried with him similar restrictions. Dokujin spent his springs in the oven, his summers at the gate, his autumns in the well, and his winters in the garden, and it was forbidden to make repairs in any of the four places until he had moved on. If repairs were absolutely necessary, the owner of the establishment had to move out by way of expiation.

This by no means means exhausts the complexities of the system. Anyone who wishes to investigate it further will find large quantities of undigested and frequently contradictory material in the *Kojiruien,* the massive official encyclopedia. There is also a detailed study in French: Bernard Frank, *Kataimi et kata-tagae: Etude sur les interdits de direction à l'époque Heian* (Paris, 1958).

Buddhism, Shinto, and divination all made their demands. There were periods of isolation brought on by Shinto pollution, there were Buddhist *nagashōji* (which I have translated "retreats") and pilgrimages to gain happiness in this incarnation and a store of virtue for the next, there were *monoimi* (which I have consistently translated "penances," although "abstinences" might sometimes be better) to make amends for breaking the diviners' proscriptions and to defend against bad omens and unfortunate developments in the horoscope. There was in short an incredibly complicated system of taboos and punishments.

Women may have taken their religion more seriously than men—there are indications in this diary that Kaneie was more than a little amused when the author "got religion"—and if they did, it was perhaps because of their unhappy and uncertain status under the Heian marriage system. It is said sometimes that Heian women were in a remarkably good position and that women's rights in Japan have been declining ever since, with perhaps a vague upsurge these last few years. In a sense this is true, since the power of the Fujiwara was based on their control through their daughters of uxorious emperors and crown princes; but connubial happiness was often denied to them by virtue of the fact that the marital state itself was so badly defined.

The *ritsuryō,* the eighth-century codes that were theoretically in effect throughout the Heian period, provided for monogamy. A clear distinction was made between wife and concubine, and stiff penalties were provided for bigamy. In practice, however, the gradations from wife to concubine to out-and-out mistress seem to have been vague. Genji went through the formalities of marriage with Murasaki, but this did not keep him from later taking the Emperor's third daughter (called Nyosan in the Waley translation of the *Tale of Genji*) for his wife. Of Kaneie's ladies, Tokihime was the principal wife while "the lady in the alley" was clearly a mistress, soon discarded. The author of this diary and the daughter of Kuniaki (the "Omi" of the diary?) on the other hand fell somewhere between. The Heian lady could and did inherit property, and she was not required to leave her childhood home immediately upon marriage—rather the gentleman entered her house and for the time being lived with or visited her there. Still the uncertainty of a badly articulated system of polygamy must have been intense. The insanity of Higekuro's wife in the *Tale of Genji* and the hysterical jealousy of Michitsuna's mother were perhaps common manifestations of the strain on the mind of the delicate Heian lady.

✳

One is hampered in trying to reconstruct the material culture of the Heian period by the fact that so little remains. There are no surviving examples of the Heian mansion, the *shinden,* and there are almost no surviving Heian temples that can be dated before the declining years of the period. The first three centuries of the Heian period in fact represent one of the principal blind spots in the study of Japanese architecture. For the more distant Nara period at least one building, the Dempōdō of the Hōryūji, remains to show what private upper-class dwellings must have been like; but for the Heian period there are only literary descriptions, a few foundation stones, and evidence from picture scrolls often painted some centuries after the incidents represented.

For what it is, in any case, the evidence points to an architecture that in its basic principles was not different from Japanese architecture today: a wooden framework, removable walls, and an emphasis on restraint and simplicity in the choice of materials and furnishings.

Unlike the modern Japanese house, the Heian mansion in its standard form was a collection of rectangular buildings laid out in a symmetrical pattern and joined by covered passageways. Each building was basically one room, although, and the tendency increased as the period drew to a close, sections were on occasion partitioned off as storerooms or withdrawing rooms.

The central building, the *shinden* proper, faced south, and was flanked on the east and west by outbuildings called the *nishi no tai* and the *higashi no tai* (see Appendix, Plate 1). Corridors were pushed out in front of the latter two buildings to join each of them to a pavilion, so that the main group of buildings and corridors formed a rectangle open to the south. The court and the open space beyond were used for the principal garden, consisting in its classical form of a lake, a pine island, a stream, one or two artificial hills, grasses, flowering plants, and white sand. Reconstructions of the Heian garden viewed from the *shinden* and from above the *shinden* are shown in Appendix, Plates 2 and 3.

One more building, a "northern wing," *kita no tai,* was customarily occupied by the principal wife, the *kita no kata.* The main *shinden* was used to receive guests and possibly as the master's living quarters. The other apartments, to which could be added as required new buildings and new connecting passages behind the main buildings, were portioned out among various other ladies, children, and attendants. In the case of the author of the *Kagerō Nikki,* it appears that, for most of the years covered by the diary, she herself was the principal occupant of the mansion. She may therefore have occupied the *shinden* proper, with Michitsuna in the east or west wing, and various relatives and guests now and then vaguely apparent in other apartments.

The *shinden*-type mansion seems to have taken on a distinctly Japanese air by the middle of the Heian period. It had curved, frequently bark-shingled roofs with deep eaves; it was raised from the ground by open wooden piling; and it had the subdued tones that continue to dominate Japanese architecture. Lacquered pillars and tiled roofs seem to have survived as a reminder, how prevalent a one it is not possible to say, of the Nara period. At one place in the diary we are told that the author's house had a tiled roof.

The interior, like that of the Japanese house today, was but sparsely furnished. The straw mats that today cover the floor of the room were in the Heian period supplied only for places where people were expected to sit. A lacquer cupboard, writing equipment, perhaps a "Chinese" box or chest in lacquer and inlay (a highly developed art in the Heian period), a pair of wooden animals guarding the *chōdai* (for which see the next paragraph), a charcoal brazier in winter, and very little else, it seems, broke the bareness of the room.

The standard unit (*shinden* proper or major outbuilding) was made up of several rectangular layers centering upon the *moya* or "mother chamber" and within that on the *chōdai,* literally the "curtain platform" (see Appendix, Plate 3). Beginning on the outside, there were the *sunoko,* an open veranda; the *hisashi,* four subsections designated as the north, the south, the east, and the west, and formed by the deep eaves; and the *moya.* The *sunoko* was separated from the *hisashi* by latticed shutters, the top half of which could be raised and anchored to the eaves, and the bottom half of which was removable; or, when the shutters were open, by bamboo or reed blinds, curtains, or possibly sliding doors. The *hisashi* were separated from the *moya* by another set of blinds, curtains, or doors. The *chōdai,* within the *moya,* was a combined bedchamber and withdrawing room, a slightly raised portion of the *moya,* covered with straw matting and surrounded by curtains.

Within all these curtains lived the Heian lady. Unless she was a lady in waiting and her duties required her to be more active, she rarely ventured beyond the veranda. She received gentleman callers, including her brothers, from behind curtains, unless she was very intimate with them, and even when she allowed them to come inside she concealed the better part of herself behind fans and curtains, and under enormous heaps of clothing.

Her basic garment was not much different from the kimono of today, though it was worn more loosely, without the wide, binding obi, and it was surmounted on formal occasions by a short, long-sleeved jacket called *karaginu* and a sort of train called *mo* (see Appendix, Plate 4) and on very formal occasions by a long, trailing shawl and sash. The principal characteristics of the lady's robes, however, were that they were much larger than she and that they were piled on layer after layer—there are records of more than twenty such layers—until she was rendered quite immobile. Sometimes she went forth on foot, when she felt called upon to make a particularly arduous pilgrimage to some nearby temple, and then she was allowed to tuck up her skirts a bit; but for the rest she stayed at home (or occasionally went out in a heavily curtained oxcart), a shapeless and almost inert bundle of clothes surmounted by a spectral white face and masses of streaming black hair.

Darkness and inaction seem thus to have set the tone of the Heian lady's life. The sun came but dimly through the deep layers of blinds and curtains, and at night the moonlight filtered in with little competition from artificial light—one is reminded of those dusky chambers in Kyoto where emperors are put to write commemorative verses after viewing a carp or planting a pine somewhere. The darkness and the immense leisure of the Heian lady's life account I think for the lack of striking tones in the best of Heian literature, for its slowness and repetitiousness, and one must ask the reader to take it at its own pace. The tears and the damp sleeves, the preoccupation with a subtle color modulation or a stroke of the brush, the sweet melancholy that so distinguishes the Heian period from the vigorous Nara period, are all comprehensible and even moving when one considers the unchanging twilight, the seclusion, the inaction that produced them.

✳

The reader who has been through three remarkable books will have had a very good introduction to what might be called the mood of Heian culture: G. B. Sansom's *History of Japan to 1334* (Stanford University Press, 1958); *Sources of the Japanese Tradition,* edited by de Bary, Tsunoda, and Keene (Columbia University Press, 1958); and Arthur Waley's translation of *The Tale of Genji* (first published complete by Allen and Unwin, London, 1935). Sansom's *Japan: A Short Cultural History* (London, Cresset, 1931; revised, 1936) has less to say about the Heian period, but it is a classic that has not been superseded by his more recent and ambitious work. Karl Florenz's *Geschichte der japanischen Literatur* (Leipzig, Amerlangs, 1906) continues to be the most detailed and Donald Keene's *Japanese Literature* (London, Murray, 1953) the most stimulating Western study of Japanese literature.

Besides Bernard Frank's study of divination (see above, page 18), the following are to be recommended for their treatment of more restricted problems: William P. Malm, *Japanese Music* (Tokyo, Tuttle, 1959); Alexander Soper, *The Evolution of Buddhist Architecture in Japan* (Princeton University Press, 1942); Robert Treat Paine and Alexander Soper, *The Art and Architecture of Japan* (London, Penguin Books, 1955); Anesaki Masaharu, *History of Japanese Religion* (London, Kegan Paul, 1930); and R. A. B. Ponsonby-Fane, *Kyoto* (Hong Kong, privately printed, 1931).

Besides the Waley translations already mentioned, important prose translations from Heian literature include the following: *The Tosa Diary* (Tosa Nikki) by Donald Keene, in his *Anthology of Japanese Literature* (New York, Grove, 1955); the *Sarashina Nikki, Murasaki Shikibu Nikki,* and *Izumi Shikibu Nikki* by Annie Shepley Omori and Kōchi Doi in *Diaries of Court Ladies of Old Japan* (Tokyo, Kenkyūsha, 1935); *The Tale of the Lady Ochikubo* (Ochikubo Monogatari) by Wilfrid Whitehouse (Kobe, Thompson, 1935); *The Pillow Book of Sei Shōnagon* (selections from the *Makura no Sōshi*) by Waley (Boston, Houghton Mifflin, 1929); *Les notes de chevet de Sei Shōnagon* (Makura no Sōshi) by André Beaujard (Paris, Maisonneuve, 1934); *The Tale of the Bamboo Cutter* (Taketori

Monogatari) by Keene (Tokyo, *Monumenta Nipponica*, IX, 4, 1956); the *Tsutsumi Chūnagon Monogatari* by Edwin O. Reischauer and Joseph K. Yamagiwa and part of the *Okagami* by Yamagiwa, in *Translations from Early Japanese Literature* (Cambridge, Harvard University Press, 1951); and the *Ise Monogatari* by Frits Vos (The Hague, Mouton, 1957).

*

Like most works of the period, this diary is full of poems. There are in fact three hundred and six short ones and three long ones, most of them not very good. I have not attempted to put them into verse, except for a very few which have of their own accord turned up with rhymes. The three long poems have been broken into short lines, and thus distinguished from the prose background by typographical arrangement if not by diction.

To indicate a poem, unless the text specifies that it is one, I have adopted the perhaps awkward device of single quotation marks within the usual double marks. Thus on page 49, the portion of the following communication which is enclosed by single quotation marks is a poem: "Right you are," he wrote again. " 'And who, among those who travel the mud-spattered way, does not get his sleeves wet in this disturbing downpour?' "

I have avoided the use of personal names. They appear but rarely in the Japanese text. I have tried, however, to apply the same designation throughout the translation to each of the principal figures. Kaneie is always "the Prince," Michitsuna "the boy," and Tokihime "the lady at the main house."

Macrons are used for long *o* and *u* in lower case, but not in capitals, in all Japanese words except the following, which are too familiar to Western readers to require them: Tokyo, Kyoto, Kyushu, Shinto.

In preparing the translation of which a revision is offered here, I became greatly indebted to Miss Oyama Atsuko, then of Tokyo University; Miss Morimoto Motoko of Ochanomizu Women's University; the late Professor Ikeda Kikan of Tokyo University; and Professor Kobayashi Shimmei of Tokyo University of Education. In the work of revision I repeatedly bothered Miss Morimoto, and she was always patient, with problems that she must have thought settled a decade earlier.

✳ On Retranslation

(from the Japan Quarterly, *Vol. VII, No. 4, October-December 1960, Asahi Shimbun Publishing Company, Tokyo)*

Eight or nine years ago I translated a tenth-century journal called the *Kagerō Nikki* or *Gossamer Diary*. I had in those days an exuberantly free notion of what a translation was, and did not mind helping my authoress when on occasion her ability to express herself seemed to falter. I did after all have the precedent of Dr. Arthur Waley, who, at least in his important translations from the Japanese, has never minded a bit of trimming here, a bit of padding there, to make his originals more coherent and pungent.

A year or so ago UNESCO told me that it would not mind sponsoring a republication of the translation, but that my exuberance had taken me altogether too far. I ought to consider reworking it. Curious to see how the translation would look now, with sober middle age in sight or even closer, and certain that without some such prodding as this I would never get around to examining it, I agreed. The reworking has been going on for some weeks now. It was delayed by the "people's movement" of May and June, which was very harassing; but now it approaches completion, and the time has come to consider whether or not the time has been well spent.

I think it has not, for a minor reason and a major reason. The first is that the original translation contains just the wrong number of mistakes. I do not think that they are sufficiently numerous to make it a bad translation, and I suspect that most translations, and know that certain translations which have become classics, contain as many. Yet they are sufficiently numerous to impress those who will make use of the *Handy Guide to Gossamer Howlers* I am providing in the retranslation. There are places where I have wild geese wintering when they should be summering, poems I have attributed to ladies when closer scrutiny shows them to be by

gentlemen, passages where a little more persistence in prob-
ing through apparently dead verbiage would have revealed
traces of life. There is one very discomfiting passage in
which, because of impatience with a garbled text, I have a
hot-blooded young man advancing. Through the mists of a
millennium, it now seems at least possible that he is retreating. The consequences are serious for the honor of the
lady to or from whom the movement takes place, and I
should have been more careful.

This is the minor reason, however. I take comfort in the
belief that those who have grappled with similar texts will
understand, and refrain from writing gleeful reviews. If they
do write such, may they one day be shamed into revisions of
their own youthful products.

The other reason is far more serious. It has to do with the
impossibility of explaining to the general reader, for whom
all of us like to think we are working, that there can be many
translations of the same passage, rather different from one
another but none of them wrong. The range of variation is
severely limited, it is true, when one is translating some
such exhortation as "No Smoking" or "Drive on the Left
in the United Kingdom and Ireland"; but it can be rather
broad when Heian Japanese is being put into English, and
this for two reasons.

In the first place, there are passages that no one really
understands, and everyone has his own view of. The diary
closes with a group of poems the authorship of which is
hopelessly obscure. Clearly they are exchanged by persons
of two sexes. The same couple, two couples, several couples? Radiant young lovers or persons bored with marriage?
If the former, the tone is clearly earnest ("sincere"); if the
latter, it must be ironic. If there are two couples, some
poems may be sincere, others ironic; and if a multitude of
couples, a person must leap back and forth with the greatest
agility between sincerity and irony. All of these interpretations are possible, and, unless someone comes up with a less
fragmentary text, no one can be sure which is correct.

No one can even be sure what the title of the diary means.
Until now there have been two theories: a *kagerō* is a delicate

kind of insect, or it is one of those refractory shimmerings you see on a warm day. Recently a gentleman has borrowed a leaf from Dr. Waley and informed us, in a new text brought out by the proud Iwanami Shoten, that *kagerō* means "gossamer." Gossamer in Webster's first sense: "A film of cobwebs floating in the air in calm, clear weather." There is no evidence that *kagerō* has ever meant this, or that the *Gossamer Diary* and its author, Lady Gossamer, are anything but products of Dr. Waley's resourceful mind. The Iwanami gentleman has stated his opinion with such firmness, however, that anyone who rejects it will no doubt be spurned by Iwanami and all its instruments.

One need have little fear that the instruments of Iwanami will get at that general reader of translations. In any case, the variations possible because of obscurities in the text are less difficult to explain than variations possible because every translator has his own idea of what he is up to. Unless a translation is hopelessly inaccurate—has people advancing all over the place when they should be retreating—it cannot be judged apart from the translator's aims. Does he wish to give literary pleasure in a translation of a work that gave literary pleasure, even if he must sometimes abandon its precise words; or does he wish to give the precise words to someone who may or may not be able to read the original himself, and may or may not be able to guess how they add up to literary pleasure? It is a very enviable translator who does not have to make the choice, and probably he does not exist among translators from classical Japanese to modern English. Dr. Waley may be taken as an example of a sensitive writer who has made the first choice, Drs. Shively, Reischauer, and Yamagiwa as examples of scrupulous scholars who have made the second.

Most of the revisions in my *Kagerō* are to be explained by the fact that, without thinking to earn for myself the characterization "scrupulous," I have wavered somewhat from Dr. Waley's pole toward that of the other three gentlemen. The literary effect of the translation no longer seems as all-important as it once did, especially since the style of the original is not always above reproach. If, to cite but one small example, everything from spring greenery to a dead parent is "touching" in the original, well, there may also be a certain monotony in the responses recorded in the translation. There may be, but the main point, and the main reason for misgivings about offering the translation to the waiting world, remains the same; everything from the products of Dr. Waley to those of the three academic gentlemen is permissible. Incompetence is not permissible, however, and inconsistency is not—starting out with a set of aims and failing to attain them or to stick by them.

Let the general reader be given a sort of touchstone.

Misgivings about the perhaps too heady freedom of the earlier translation seem to have been based largely on the first paragraph. It happens that the first paragraph is one of the vaguest and yet most pathetically effective in the whole diary. Eight years ago I thought to start off with a wallop. The pity of things would be there, however cavalier the treatment of the specific words. The tenth century would be made to speak directly to the twentieth century.

Here, with fairly scrupulous literalness, is one of the more puzzling remarks in that paragraph: "She thought that she would write even of her own not-human position, and people would think it strange, and it would be an example for those who asked: 'The well-placed people of the world?'"

In the original translation it comes out thus: "Perhaps, I think to myself, the events of my own life, if I were to put them down in a journal, might attract attention, and indeed those who have been misled by the romancers might find in it a description of what the life of a well-placed lady is really like."

In the new translation it will probably be something like this: "Perhaps, she said to herself, even the story of her own dreary life, set down in a journal, might be of interest, and it might also answer a question: had that life been one befitting a well-born lady?"

Both amplifications of that enigmatic question seem valid, and certainly some amplification is necessary. I now favor the latter because it contains the stronger touch of self-pity, and is therefore more in keeping with the mood of the whole. ''Lady Gossamer'' is not one to make her point by restraint and discreet withdrawal. She comes right out and asks for tears when she wants them.

But though I now favor the second, the choice is not an easy one to make. It requires a fundamental decision on how much the translator may tamper with the words of the original to avoid lowering its worth—affronting its dignity, so to speak. Self-pity is not and has not been considered as reprehensible an emotion in Japan as it is considered in the West. Never were there louder sobs of it than in such Kabuki plays as *Sendai-hagi* and *Terakoya,* and the greatest figure in Japanese literature, the Shining Genji, is always sighing over himself.

Quite simply, this note of self-pity cannot have had the effect on the tenth-century reader of Japanese that it has on the twentieth-century reader of English. Should the passage then be toned down so that, though he loses the words that are probably nearest the original sense, the reader does not take it in the wrong spirit? Or should he be asked to accommodate himself a little to his tenth-century authoress? Should he be told that this is how she was, and that, being the child of a most alien tradition, he must not ask her to be different?

One would have thought that in the retranslation my choice was made in that first paragraph, and must be final. Unfortunately these choices are not easy to stand by, and if I began moving in the direction of the three scrupulous professors, the sharp-eyed reader will find me from time to time wandering back in the direction of Dr. Waley. A chuckle at some particularly cunning excision or interpolation, a brief bout of conscience, a murmur of conviction that my authoress would not have wished it otherwise—and the translation has gone unrevised. The inconsistency is more reprehensible than the mistakes, and potential reviewers, those who take their duties seriously, are warned to be on the watch for it.

*
 * *The Gossamer Years*
 *
  *

✳ *Book One*

THESE times have passed, and there was one who drifted uncertainly through them, scarcely knowing where she was. It was perhaps natural that such should be her fate. She was less handsome than most, and not remarkably gifted. Yet, as the days went by in monotonous succession, she had occasion to look at the old romances, and found them masses of the rankest fabrication. Perhaps, she said to herself, even the story of her own dreary life, set down in a journal, might be of interest; and it might also answer a question: had that life been one befitting a well-born lady? But they must all be recounted, events of long ago, events of but yesterday. She was by no means certain that she could bring them to order.

✳ *The Eighth Year of Tenryaku (954)*

I SHALL not touch upon the frivolous love notes I had received from time to time. Now the Prince[1] was beginning to send messages. Most men would have gone through a suitable intermediary, a lady in waiting perhaps, but he went directly to my father with hints, possibly half-joking at first, that he would like to marry me; and even after I had indicated how inappropriate I found the idea he sent a mounted messenger to pound on my gate. I scarcely needed to ask who it was. With the house in an uproar, I finally had to take the message, though I would have preferred to refuse it. My women only became noisier.

It consisted of but one verse: "Sad am I, 'mid talk about the warbler. May not I too hear its voice?"

The paper was rather unbecoming for such an occasion, I thought, and the handwriting was astonishingly bad. Having heard that he was a most accomplished penman, I wondered indeed whether he might not have had someone else write it.

I was half-inclined not to answer, but my mother[2] insisted that a letter from such a gentleman was not to be ignored, and finally I sent off a return poem: "Let no bird waste its song in a wilderness where it finds no answer."

That was the beginning. There came other poems, but I let them go unanswered. There was this, for instance: "Shall I liken you to the noiseless waterfall of Yamashiro? And when, I wonder, do we come to the pleasanter shallows?"[3] I continued to turn his messengers back with promises that I would answer later, until my mother was aroused to action by this piece of doggerel:

"Perhaps now, perhaps now, I whisper to myself. But you do not answer. I am left desolate."

"You cannot continue to ignore such a man," she said. "You must stop being so kittenish."

And so I had one of my ladies compose a poem, suitable but hardly warm, and even at this secondhand reply he seemed delighted. I was besieged with poems. One of them suggested that my failure to write my own letters probably told of other and more interesting suitors:

"The plover's tracks are gone from the beach. Is it that the waves are higher now?" This too I answered by proxy.

"The sincere tone of your notes is as I would have it," he remarked at the end of one rather earnest letter, "but if you persist in having someone else write them I must conclude that you are heartless. 'Two of you there are, and I hesitate to choose between you; but let me now hear from her who has scorned to show herself.'"[4]

Still I declined to answer directly, and we continued to correspond on into the autumn without entering into a more serious relationship. And then I finally sent my own reply to this one:

"I suspect that someone is interfering. I have tried to remain calm, but how is it that, 'though my village lies quiet, untroubled by the calls of the night-wooing deer, my nights are sleepless?'"

"This last statement of yours is indeed strange," I answered. " 'Even in the mountains above Takasago, one hears, they sleep well despite the deer.' "

And again, somewhat later, he wrote:

The barrier of Osaka, the gate to pleasant meetings,[5]
Is so very near and yet, alas, so difficult to cross.

I answered with a similar word play:

Well may you speak of Osaka, which summons and forbids.
But what of famous Nakoso, that Barrier "Come-not-my-way?"[6]

And so the letters went, and then one morning—when might it have been?[7]—he sent me this verse: "Like the River Oi awaiting a flow of logs, my tears pour on as I await the eve."

And I answered: " 'Countless as the logs upon the Oi are my misgivings; and, try though I may to stop them, my tears outflow the river.' "[8]

Two mornings later came another poem: "I was swept away like the dew in the rising sun; and my heart seemed to die within me."

Again my answer: " 'Powerless as the dew—how wretched that must be. But think of me, more feeble yet, made to rely on the dew!' "

The days went by. He came to visit me one evening when, for certain reasons, I was away from home, but he went back early the following morning and left behind this note: "I had hoped to spend at least today with you, but the indications are that this would not be convenient. Have you left me and become a hermit?"

I answered with but one verse: "The wild carnation in the alien hedge is broken and can no longer support the dew."[9]

Toward the end of the Ninth Month[10] he stayed away for two nights running and sent only a very hasty note by way of explanation. I replied in verse:

My sleeves still wet from last night's dew—then why
Must I wake to find another cloudy sky?

He sent back immediately:

Cloudy indeed. And shall I tell you why?

'Tis my troubled thoughts reflected in the sky.

He appeared before I had time to finish my answer.

Time passed. One rainy day, when I had not seen him for some time, he sent a messenger (or so I remember it) to say that he would visit me that evening.

" 'In vain they look to the oak for protection,' " I answered. " 'Night after night the rain drips through on the grasses under the grove.' "[11]

He came immediately, no doubt to avoid the bother of having to compose an answer.

Part of the Tenth Month I spent in penance,[12] and this seemed to annoy him.

" 'The sleeve of my turned-out robe is chill with tears,' " he wrote, " 'and this morning even the heavens seem to weep.' "

I answered: " 'Ah, but when one really loves, the warmth of one's thoughts should dry those turned-out sleeves.' "[13]

But my effort seemed a bit trite and old-fashioned.

And then, just at the gloomiest time of the year, my father left for a post in the far north. My last meetings with him were sad ones. The Prince seemed aware of my unhappiness and vowed that he would never desert me, but I had doubts about the reliability of human affections and did not really feel that our relations had progressed to the point where I could depend on him.

The day set for my father's departure came. He was unable to hold back his tears, and my own grief I find quite impossible to describe. He lingered at the threshold, even after his attendants had pointed out that he was behind schedule. Finally he thrust a note into my writing box and rushed from the house weeping uncontrollably.

For a moment I could not bring myself to see what he had written. But he was really gone, and, hesitantly, I took out his note. It was a poem, apparently addressed to the Prince: "I depart for the northern outposts, I have only you to rely on; may your journey with her be a long one, as mine must be alone." My tears welled up afresh, and I put the note back into the box for the Prince to find.

He came almost immediately, but I refused to let him see my face. "What is the matter with you?" he protested. "It is a common enough thing for officials to go off to the provinces, and this only indicates that you do not trust me."

Then he found the poem, and he too was much moved by it. He sent out an answering verse to my father, whose party had stopped for the night:[14] "You shall come back to see a faith enduring as the pines of Sue no Matsuyama, dry above the threatening waves."[15]

The days passed, and I continued to feel pangs of loneliness at the thought of my father off on his long journey. The Prince showed little prospect of becoming the reliable support we had hoped. In the Twelfth Month he made a pilgrimage to Yogawa[16] and sent word that he was unable to come down because of the snow. I sent back a verse: "Even the snow has more to sustain it than I—for it falls on a frozen Yogawa."

Swiftly the year came to a close.

* The Ninth Year of Tenryaku (955)

EARLY in the new year I went off on a short journey. I had not seen him for two or three days, and I left this verse to be delivered if he should call: "Unwanted, I go out to cry on the moor with the song thrush."[17]

Presently he answered: "'Your call will summon me, though frivolity explain this wandering the wilds with the thrush.'"

It had meanwhile become clear that I was to have a child. I passed a most unpleasant spring and summer and toward the end of the Eighth Month gave birth to a boy. The Prince showed every sign of affection.

But the following month I received a shock. Toying with my writing box one morning just after he had left, I came upon a note obviously intended for another woman. My chagrin was infinite, and I felt that I must at least let him know I had seen the thing. "'Might it be a bill of divorcement,'" I wrote, "'this note that I see for another?'"

As the weeks went by, my anxiety increased. Toward the

end of the Tenth Month he stayed away three nights running, and when he finally appeared he explained nonchalantly that he had hoped by ignoring me for a few days to find out what my feelings really were.[18] But he could not stay the night: he had an appointment, he said, which could not very well be broken. I was of course suspicious, and I had him trailed. I found that he spent the night in a house off a certain narrow side street. It was so, then, I thought. My worst suspicions were confirmed.

Two or three days later I was awakened toward dawn by a pounding on the gate. It was he, I knew, but I could not bring myself to let him in, and presently he went off, no doubt to the alley that interested him so.

I felt that I could not let things stand as they were. Early the next morning I sent, attached to a withered chrysanthemum, a poem written with more care than usual: "Do you know how slow the dawn can be when you have to wait alone?"[19]

"I had intended to wait at your gate until sunrise," he replied, "but I was called away on urgent business. You are right to be annoyed, and yet—'though perhaps not as stubborn as a winter's dawn, an unopened gate means cruel waiting too.'"

And so he pretended that there was nothing unnatural about his behavior, nothing at which I could take offense; but I found his glibness quite distasteful and wished that he had the courtesy to hide his new affair somewhat more cleverly, perhaps to keep it out of sight for a while, as he could very easily have done, under the cloak of court business.

✳ *The Tenth Year of Tenryaku (956)*

IN THE Third Month came the Festival of the Peach Blossoms.[20] We had our decorations ready, and I rather expected him to come for a look at them; and my sister's husband,[21] who was so devoted, we knew would come too. But the day passed, and we had no guests.

Then early the following morning both of them called.

Our people had been waiting for them since the day before and, apparently on the theory that there was no point in seeing the day's effort go entirely to waste, began breaking off the blossoms that had been saved for him and bringing them from the inner apartments.

I felt a sudden wave of annoyance as I watched them, and, taking my brush, I wrote down a verse as though I were but practicing: "We had them for you yesterday. What good do you do coming around today?" But what was the use, I said to myself, and made as if to hide what I had written. He was quick to notice and seized the paper from me. He added an answering verse: "Our love is as lasting as the tree that bears fruit but once in thirty centuries;[22] are we to pause each year over these trivial annuals?"

And my sister's husband too wrote an apology: " 'We stayed away purposely: we would not have it thought that we love you for your flower arrangements.' "

The Prince's visits to the alley meanwhile came out quite into the open, and it even appeared at times that he had become somewhat restive in his relations with the lady in the main house.[23] My own anguish was intense, but there was after all little I could do about it.

My sister continued to receive her husband regularly. Before long, however, he began to find the atmosphere of the place oppressive and took her away to a house where, he said, he could visit her in somewhat lighter spirits. My gloom increased. I would not see her again, I thought, and as the carriage came to take her away I handed her a poem: "The wailing groves round my mansion flourish, and only mankind languishes."

Her husband wrote the answer: " 'Do not put with his fickle words these words of a steadfast admirer.' "

With that they drove off, and thereafter, as I had foreseen, I spent my days and nights alone. Life for the most part was not uncomfortable; it was simply that the Prince's behavior left me chronically dissatisfied. And I was apparently not the only one thus troubled: the lady in the main house, I heard, was also being neglected. We had occasionally exchanged notes, and on the Third or Fourth Day of the Fifth Month I sent her this verse: "If the marsh grass is missing from your garden too, in what swamp is it rooted this time?"[24]

She replied: "'The grass is missing—that much is true—but I had thought it was your marsh that claimed it.'"

The first part of the Sixth Month was rainy. "The underleaves of these sad trees have faded," I added to my other poems, "even as I have watched them through this long rain."[25]

He appeared one evening in the Seventh Month, and I refused to speak to him. I had begun to feel that it would be better for him to leave off seeing me entirely than to continue his irregular and unenthusiastic visits. One of my ladies undertook to cover the silence and mentioned among other things my poem about the unseasonal fading of the leaves.

"'But if they are changing color even now,'" he wrote in reply, "'think how much richer they will be when the autumn comes.'"

And I took up my brush to protest: "'The colored leaves are but sadder, unwanted in the autumn.'"[26]

He continued to come now and then, but none of his visits could be called pleasant. Each indeed seemed more trying than the one before. Sometimes, seeing that I was again in a bad mood, he would leave early to avoid my attack,[27] and once a person[28] who lived near me and saw what was happening felt called upon to speak of his hurried exits: "'It sputters and smokes like a salt-maker's fire,[29] this fire in the quarrelsome heart.'" Thus our relations came to attract unwelcome attention.

His visits became still more infrequent. I began to feel listless and absent-minded as I had never been before,[30] and I fell into the habit of overlooking things I had left lying around the house. "Perhaps he has given me up completely," I would say to myself, "and has he left behind nothing to remember him by?" And then, after an interval of about ten days, I received a letter asking me to send him the arrow attached to the bed[31] pillar. He had indeed left behind that much—I remembered now.

I returned it with a poem: "I am aroused by this call for

an arrow, even as I wonder what is to bring memories."[32]

My house was directly on his way to and from the palace, and in the night or early in the morning I would hear him pass. He would cough to attract my attention. I wanted not to hear, but, tense and unable to sleep, and making the long nights longer, I would listen for his approach. If only I could live where I would not be subjected to this, I thought over and over. And I would hear my women talking among themselves of his current indifference—"He used to be so fond of her," they would say—and my wretchedness would increase as night came on again.

I heard once more that the lady in the main house was being neglected. She had several children, and her plight I thought was even sadder than mine. In about the Ninth Month I wrote her a letter of condolence, including this verse: "The spider's trail is lost in the empty sky; but perhaps I may trust the winds to ask of you."[33]

She answered courteously: "'It is a question of an inconstant heart. Are the autumn winds to be trusted with the changing autumn leaves?'"

I saw him now and then as the winter drew on; he was not prepared to break with me finally, it seemed. For the rest I spent my time with the child, and, though I should have preferred not to, I would find myself murmuring, "How I should like to ask the fish, even them, why he neglects me."[34]

✳ *The First Year of Tentoku (957)*

THE NEW year came, and spring. Once he sent a girl to pick up a book he had left at my house, and I wrote this on the wrapping: "'Wasted is the beach where the plover left his tracks; and wasted too is the heart.'"[35]

His reply was glib: "'Wasted the heart, you say—but it is certainly not that the plover has found a better place for his tracks.'"

And I retorted: "'To find the tracks you speak of, I should have to search along strands boundless as my sorrows.'"

Summer came, and a child was born to his paramour. Loading the lady into his carriage and raising a commotion that could be heard through the whole city, he came hurrying past my gate[36]—in the worst of taste, I thought. And why, my women loudly asked one another, had he so pointedly passed our gate when he had all the streets in the city to choose from? I myself was quite speechless and thought only that I would like to die on the spot. I knew that I would be capable of nothing drastic, but I resolved not to see him again.

Three or four days later I received a most astonishing letter: "I have not been able to see you because we have been having rather a bad time of it here. Yesterday the child was born, however, and everything seems to have gone well. I know that you will not want to see me until the defilement has worn off."

I dismissed the messenger without a reply. The child, I heard, was a boy, and that news of course made me feel even worse.

He came calling three or four days later quite as though nothing unusual had happened. I refused even to look at him, and shortly he left. Similar incidents occurred more than once after that.

In the Seventh Month, at about the time of the wrestling meet,[37] he sent over material for two sets of robes and asked me to have them sewn. I discussed the matter with my mother.

"This is very fine," she said. "Over where he is playing these days, there is probably no one who can sew a stitch. That is what happens when you go around collecting noisy, incompetent females."[38]

The cleverer of my women agreed that he was being most tiresome. "We will surely hear what a bungle they have made of it." Indeed we did hear, after we sent them back, that the robes had to be farmed out widely in search of competent seamstresses.

Perhaps he found us perverse. He stayed away for more than twenty days; and then, I do not remember exactly when, I had a letter: "I should like to visit you, but your behavior rather discourages me. Tell me clearly that you would like to see me and I shall come, though with some hesitation.''

I thought I would not answer, but my women argued that that would be cruel indeed, and finally I sent a single verse: ''Perhaps it would be best to follow whatever grass plumes beckon.''[39]

He replied by return messenger: '' 'When the grasses wave in the east wind, "Come this way," then surely I will follow.' ''[40]

I sent back another poem: ''What good can the grasses do, putting out their plumes in the harsh autumn winds?''[41]

So things went and presently he appeared, but we felt the usual constraint. He lay looking out at the garden—the flowers in the foreground were just then in full bloom—and wrote down a verse: ''Is it but the soft covering of dew that makes these colors flash so wildly?'' And I answered: '' 'These flowers must face the autumn—you should know their wildness has that deeper source.' ''

It was toward the end of the month, and the late moon was just coming out when he began to show signs of leaving. ''But perhaps I should stay. ...'' he remarked tentatively, as though something in my manner indicated that I hoped he would. But I did not want him to think I was detaining him, and taking my brush I wrote a verse: ''If the moon takes upon itself to launch out into the sky, who am I to stop it?''

'' 'Intent though it be on its flight through the sky, the moon leaves a shadow upon the waters,' '' he replied. ''If you want me to stay, I shall stay.'' And he did.

That autumn we had rather a violent storm, and two days later he called. ''Most people,'' I remarked, ''would have sent to find out how I was coming through the storm.'' He may have seen the justice in my complaint, but he rolled off a poem with complete nonchalance: ''Better that I have come as my own courier. The winds would have scattered my message.''

And I took up the game: '' 'It might have scattered your words, but still it was a friendly east wind, blowing my way.' ''[42]

He pressed the argument with another verse: "Am I to trust such a message to a foolish east wind? Think of the rumors it might have spread!"

But finally I had the last word: "'Very well, let us grant your point. And why do you not ask, now that you have come?'"

Once, in about the Tenth Month, an unusually violent rainstorm began just as he was getting ready to leave on "unavoidable" business.

> The winter rains will come, I know;
>
> But so late at night—and must you go?

But, paying no attention to my verse, he left. Has anyone ever been more outrageously insulted?

✳ *The Second Year of Tentoku (958)* *to the Second Year of Owa (962)*[43]

IT BEGAN to appear that the lady in the alley had fallen from favor since the birth of her child. I had prayed, at the height of my unhappiness, that she would live to know what I was then suffering, and it seemed that my prayers were being answered. She was alone, and now her child was dead, the child that had been the cause of that unseemly racket. The lady was of frightfully bad birth—the unrecognized child of a rather odd prince,[44] it was said. For a moment she had been able to use a person[45] who was unaware of her shortcomings, and now she was abandoned. The pain must be even sharper than mine had been. I was satisfied.

The Prince had moved back to his main house,[46] I heard but I saw him as rarely as ever. The child, who was beginning to talk, took to imitating the words with which his father always left the house: "I'll come again soon, I'll come again," he would chant, rather stumbling in the effort. I was sharply conscious of my loneliness as I listened to him. My nights too were lonely; there was indeed no time when I was completely happy.

My officious neighbor took it upon herself to sympathize. "You are still young," she would say, "and it hardly seems right that you should have to go on this way." But it was impossible to talk to the Prince himself. "Have I done something wrong?" he would ask innocently, and his injured and guileless manner made it impossible for me to speak. I became obsessed with the problem of how to approach him. I longed to tell him in detail how I felt. But thoughts only stormed through my head, and I could say nothing.

Then I hit on the idea of putting everything into a poem.[47]

I must ask you:
Am I to go on, restless and unhappy,
As I am now, and as I long have been,
For all my days?
Your words, that autumn we met, soon changed their
    color,
Like the leaves of the wailing grove where I must dwell.
Then my father was off among the winter clouds,
And my tears boiled up like a sudden winter storm.
He sought your promise never to forsake me.
"What foolish fears!" I thought.
But soon the white clouds came between us too.
Blankly, I watched. You were gone like the morning
    mists.
The geese come home in their time, I thought, and I
    waited,
And waited in vain, and am waiting now, the hollow
    shell of a locust.
My tears are not a flow of but this moment.
For long years now they have surged, a steady river
Whose source you are, and your inconstancy.
My load of sin from other lives is heavy,
Else why should I drag myself on, unable finally
To forsake this wretched world?
I value life no more than a bubble upon the water.
Still, I must wait for him who is far in the north,[48]
For the grasses that come to the hills, there in the
    north,
For the Abukuma[49] meeting.
One brief meeting, then forsake the world?
But regret would be too strong, I would weep again.
I was not meant to live a life of tears.

There was a time when nothing came between us,
You and me; and should I leave the world,
Memory would cancel out the profit,
And I would weep again.
Thus I think of him and think of you,
And dust piles round your unused pillow, myriad,
But myriads more the nights I spend alone.
I tell myself, for all that, not to think you are gone.
After that storm you came[50]—remember?—and as
    quickly went.
"I'll come again" became a nursery song—
Empty words of comfort. The child believed them.
"I'll come," he says again. "I'll come, I'll come."
With the chant, my tears flood up, a dreary ocean.
What must they think who are luckless enough to see?
I may be abandoned. No help for me,
A strand to which not even the seaweed comes.
But still there was your promise—"While I live"—
And if ever you come again I must try again
    To ask, to understand.

I laid it on an open shelf when I had finished it. He called after the usual interval, but I refused to see him, and presently, no doubt somewhat uncomfortable, he took the poem and left. I received this answer:

True, the newly gathered leaves will fade.
Love is but love. Each autumn is the same.
And yet (with your father's words) their color deep-
    ened,
The frost-touched underleaves of your sighing grove.
I did not forget, my purpose was as always.
I sought to see the child, and was turned away.
Like the waves that break on Tago in Suruga,
I was frowned upon by a mountain, a smoldering Fuji,
Wreathed in clouds of smoke.
The women you kept about you stood between us,[51]
They told you I would not come, they would not have
    me,
They drove me away to other, kinder places.
But sometimes still I came, and I slept alone,

And when I awoke in the middle of the night,
I found the friendly moon, quite unreserved,
And not a trace of you.
Thus one may find that love has lost its flavor,
And left one inattentive.
And where is the harem with which you have adorned
     me?
You tell me I am fickle, you press me to say
Which of my loves is the loveliest. Surely here
Is the heavy crime you speak of.
Do not wait for the Abukuma meeting.
Go now—find someone who will cherish you
As you deserve. I am not made of stone.
I shall not block your plans.
And when we part, and your tears flow like a river,
Perhaps the thought of days when we were one
Will furnish heat to dry them.
The horse upon the moor of Hemi in Kai
Is not to be restrained when once gone wild.
But what, I wonder sadly, of the colt,
     Fatherless, untended, sadly neighing?

A messenger happened to be going his way, and I sent a short poem by way of answer: "Is the horse of Michinoku to be left all its days untended by him who should tend it?"

I do not know exactly what he had in mind, but he sent this reply: "'Were I the wild horse of Obuchi, I should of course be out of hand; but since I am not ...'"[52]

And again I answered: "'The rope continues to pull, but the pony seems more reluctant.'"[53]

And he: "'The pony balks at the barrier of Shirakawa, and many days elapse along the way'—but day after tomorrow we should reach the barrier at Osaka."[54]

This was written on the Fifth Day of the Seventh Month, while he was undergoing a long penance. "'You speak of the Seventh,'" I answered; "'and do you say that I am to be content with meetings as rare as those of the stars?'"[55]

Perhaps he saw my point. For a time he seemed kinder, and so the months went by.

Meanwhile I had considerable satisfaction from reports

that the lady in the alley, the one whose activities had so upset me, was herself in rather a frenzy now that the Prince had
left her. Things were of course still far from perfect, but as
I turned the problem over and over in my mind, I concluded
that my unhappiness was part of my inescapable destiny, determined from former lives, and must be accepted as such.

And then there came a somewhat happier period. The
Prince finished his term on the Council of State and was promoted to the fourth rank, and his services at the Inner Court
were discontinued.[56] Some months later, on the annual
lists, he was made deputy head of a most unattractive ministry.[57] The post was so distasteful that he quite ignored his
official duties and spent his time on more interesting projects, and sometimes we had two and three days together in
pleasant idleness.

The Minister, his superior,[58] sent over a poem asking why
the Prince never came to the office: "Threads in the same
skein. Why then do they not meet?" The Prince replied:
"'How sad to be told that being of the same skein should
mean so little.'" The Minister followed with a second
poem, pursuing the silk-reeling figure: "It is proper to take
in silk while the summer is high; and while we are tending
to our two and three strands, the time somehow slips by."[59]

"'And is one's time to be taken up by a poor two and
three strands?'" the Prince replied. "'Count mine rather
as the seven white skeins of the old song.'"[60]

The Minister promptly apologized for underestimating
the range of the Prince's activities, and added a poem to his
letter: "Let us part without rancor, you and I, to pursue
these white threads."[61] He was in penance, he said, and
could write no more.

The Prince answered: "'But as the years go by, unpleas-
antnesses will arise from those white threads.'"[62]

Toward the end of the Fifth Month the Prince and I moved
to my father's house (he was still away in the provinces) to
begin a forty-five-day penance.[63]

The Minister was staying at a neighboring estate. We were
all kept inside by heavy rains which lasted on into the following month, and the house, rather a poor one, had a leaky

roof. At the height of our distress, the Minister sent over a poem that struck us as rather perverse: "The long, dreary rains—but the sound of the dripping is pleasant."

And we replied: "'How, submerged in this long rain, could a person find time for such wit?'"

"Right you are," he wrote again. "'And who, among those who travel the mud-spattered way, does not get his sleeves wet in this disturbing downpour?'"[64]

And the Prince returned: "'And those who regularly follow the muddy path have few nights to dry their sleeves.'"

The Minister came back again: "'It is you, the irregular, whose sleeves should be wet; where one stays regularly there is no worry about the muddy way.'"[65]

We read this last poem together, and thought him something of a rogue. Then, during a pause in the rain, the Prince went for a visit to the Lady Tokihime's, and while he was gone a letter came from the Minister. The messenger insisted that he had instructions to deliver it in spite of the Prince's absence. It began with a poem: "Do you not notice me standing by your hedge, trying to find solace for my eternal longing?[66]—but I know it is useless, and I shall leave."

When the Prince came back several days later, I showed the Minister's note to him. He decided that it was too late for an answer, and instead sent to ask why we had had no letters lately.

The Minister answered: "'The water rises and the strand disappears; is the plover lost in the rain?'—I think my letter must have gone astray, and it is hardly fair of you to suggest that I have not written. May I really expect to see you?"[67] It was written in a lady's hand,[68] something of a relief—a man's could have been so difficult.

The Prince sent a return poem: "To find those lost tracks, we must wait for the waves to recede—but that too will be hard."

And again a poem came from the Minister: "'Wait for the waves indeed—a frank and generous poem I sent, and this is the way you taunt me!'[69] There is a misunderstanding here."

The Sixth Month passed, and the purification[70] seems to have been observed at court as usual. The fortieth day of my penance must have come on about the eve of Tanabata.[71] For some time I had been troubled by a painful cough, some sort of possession[72] it appeared, against which incantations might perhaps be effective; and then it was most uncomfortable in the city during the hot season, and the Prince decided to take me off to a mountain temple not far away, one where I had been several times before.[73] On the Fifteenth and Sixteenth came the Festival of the Dead.[74] The busy crowds of votaries, with offerings in their arms or on their heads, were entirely delightful—the Prince and I watched them together. My long penance over and my health and spirits mended, we went back to the city, and the year passed, as the years will, quickly and uneventfully.

✳ *The Third Year of Owa (963)*

THE NEW year too began uneventfully. I had his full attention, and when that was the case everything was pleasant. Early in the year he was readmitted to the Inner Court.

On the day of the purification for the Kamo Festival[75] the Minister sent a letter suggesting that, if the Prince was going to the ceremony, perhaps they could ride together. Included was a poem: "My years..."[76] He was, it seemed, not at his usual residence, and the Prince went first to the side street where we supposed him to be, and, as he came out, sent this over to him: "'Spring has been unduly late here to the south of your street, but now at length, we meet it.'" The two of them went off together.

Some time later, after the Minister had returned to his principal mansion, the Prince visited him and saw again the flowers he had so admired the year before,[77] and with them plumed grasses, graceful and slender. He asked if we might have some of the grasses when they were dug up for separating. Several days later, as the two of us were going off to the river for purification,[78] we passed what I was told was the Minister's mansion. The Prince sent in a messenger to announce to whoever happened to be on duty there that he would like to call but, because he was with someone, could not, and to see what might have happened to the grasses he had asked for. The purification was quickly over, and when we returned home we were given a long box that had been sent from the Minister's. In it were the grasses, neatly dug and planted, and attached to them a poem on a bit of blue paper: "How it pains me to dig up grasses which, when they put out their plumes, will beckon pleasant guests."

We thought this most clever of him and wrote a reply which unfortunately I have forgotten. And as I think about it, I wonder what other poems I have included that I might better have forgotten.[79]

✳ *The First Year of Kōhō (964)*

SPRING passed and summer came on, and I began to feel that he was spending too many evenings at court. He would come early and pass the day with me, and then toward evening would leave "for court." It was most suspicious. One evening—it was the day I heard the *higurashi,* the "day-long cicada,"[80] for the first time—I wrote this poem as he was about to start out: "How strange. I hear the day-long cicada, but what about the night?" That apparently made it difficult for him to leave.

There was still nothing on which I could really focus my suspicions. I went on watching.[81]

One moonlit evening we were carrying on our usual joyless conversation. He said a number of rather appealing things, but I was taken with memories of happier evenings. " 'The moon on a cloudy night,' " I whispered, " 'is it more certain of its destiny than I of mine?' "

He answered half-jokingly, " 'You can rely on me—I alone know: the moon even on a cloudy night is going toward the west.' "

Thus he seemed to assure me of his dependability; but the place he called home was obviously not here, and our relationship was far from what I would have had it. And because his affections were held by others more fortunate, I still had but the one child. Indeed my life was rich only in loneliness and sorrow.

Early in the autumn my mother died. I had managed somehow to hold myself together while she was alive, but my wretchedness now was something few people know. I of all the family had been most attached to her, and I had hoped and prayed that I should not survive her. Now she was dead. For a time it seemed that my prayer would be answered—I quite lost control of my arms and legs, and felt that I must even stop breathing.

It was in a mountain temple that this happened, and the Prince, to whom I should have had to entrust my funeral arrangements, was in the city. "It appears that I may die," I said with a great effort, calling my son to my side. "Please tell your father that he is to go to no trouble for me, but ask him instead to mourn for my mother. Her own relatives will of course take care of the funeral, but I should like him to arrange something beyond what they are able to—ah, what is to be done?" I could say no more.

My mother's illness had been a long one, and most of the family had come to accept her death ahead of time. They wept over me instead, milling about and suggesting all sorts of possible remedies. I was unable to speak. Finally my father came up and forced me to take some medicine. "You have one parent left, after all," he said. "Pull yourself together." Shortly afterward I regained control of myself.

What made me wish more than anything that I had died with my mother was the memory of her sorrow during those last days. She had tried to talk but could only grieve silently, day and night. Toward the end, she murmured over and over again, hesitantly and painfully, "Ah, what is to become of you?"

The Prince came to inquire after me while I was still half delirious. One of my attendants received him and described my condition.

He was moved to tears. At first he seemed to care little about my defilement, but, cautioned by one of my women, he reconsidered and remained standing to protect himself against it.[82] He was most kind and sympathetic.

With many to help, the funeral rites were completed, and afterwards we stayed on for a time in the mountains. Life was quiet and monotonous. I was quite unable to sleep and spent my nights in mourning, and as I would look out on the mountain and see the mists closing it off, I would think how I too seemed to be shut off from help. If I went back to the city, where would I find peace? It would be better to die here, I thought—but then what would happen to the boy?[83]

Toward the middle of the month[84] I heard one of the priests, in an interval between prayers, describe a place called Mimiraku,[85] where the dead were to be seen in the distance but vanished if one approached too near. How I would like to go there, I thought: "'Even the sound of your name gives relief, O Isle of Mimiraku; let me enjoy too, if but from a distance, the visual pleasure you offer.'" My brother heard and was deeply moved: "'I hear but rumors —let me see her whom you hide, O Isle of Mimiraku.'"

The Prince came again to ask after me. Standing all the while,[86] he talked at great and troublesome length of the difficulties of defilement and such, but I remember little of what he said. I was absorbed in my grief and paid no attention to him.

There was no particular reason for me to return to the city, but the decision was not mine to make, and the day came for all of us to leave. I thought of the road up to the mountains, and how I had held my mother in my arms and exhausted myself trying to make her comfortable. But there was some hope then that she might recover, and I took strength from the thought. Now, going back, I had a fine wide carriage in which to enjoy myself, but the trip without her was a desolate one.

At home the loneliness was still sharper. The flowers we had cared for together had been allowed to go untrimmed when she fell ill, and now they were blooming in the rankest profusion. Everyone else bustled about after the necessary memorials and offerings, but I could only sit and gaze at the neglected garden. "'Left all untended, still they have flour-ished, these flowers washed by the dew of your blessing,'" I murmured, and I thought of the old poem: "The tuft of grass you planted is now an autumn moor, loud with a re-quiem of insects."[87]

My relatives were not of particularly high rank, and they stayed with me for the period of purification.[88] There was much moving of screens and curtains as each shut himself off from the rest, but I remained outside the general activity. From the first sound of prayers in the evening all through the long night, I would lie awake weeping.

The forty-ninth-day rites[89] were conducted with the whole family present. The Prince apparently took care of most of the arrangements, and the attendance was conse-quently large. I had a painting of the Buddha done as my own particular offering. After the ceremony the family separated and I was left alone. Nothing, I thought, could relieve my loneliness. The Prince, possibly aware of how I felt, came more frequently than he had been in the habit of doing.

Quite dazed with grief, I put away the things we, my mother and I, had thrown together when we started for the temple—the articles she used every day and a few letters. In the process I came on the robe the priest had thrown over her when, as she grew weaker, she was given the tonsure.[90] Shortly afterwards she died and the robe somehow was packed with her other belongings. Early one morning I pre-pared it to send back to the priest. I began a note to go with it, but I got no farther than "This robe" when I was blinded with tears. "Because of your robe," I began again, "'She has become the dew on the leaf of the lotus; but this morn-ing it is washed with another sort of dew.'"

I had asked that priest's brother, also a priest, to pray for my mother, and I heard now that he had suddenly taken ill and died. How must the surviving brother feel, I thought, and why must those on whom I depended die so quickly? I sent several messages of condolence, among them this one after the forty-ninth-day rites (the dead man was a priest of some stature in the Unrin-in): "'I did not dream that he would leave that cloudy grove to ascend the heavens as the smoke.' ''[91] I myself was still quite distraught with grief, and indeed my heart "wandered lost over hills and mountains, seeking a hermit's retreat."[92] I was living with my brother and an aunt who had taken the place of my mother, but even with her beside me I continued to mourn the past. And so the autumn and winter went by.

✳ *The Second Year of Kōhō (965)*

FOR THE anniversary of my mother's death we went again to the mountain temple where she died, and the memories were sharp. A priest warned us that we were not there to enjoy the mountain autumn but rather "to try to understand the sutras in the temple where she closed her eyes." But I was not up to the effort; I remember nothing else. We returned and went out of mourning, and, as I had all the dull mourning robes purified and even the fan, I murmured to myself (I let no one hear): "'The mourning robes are cleansed with tears, a river outflowing its banks.' ''[93]

I took out my *koto*[94] and listlessly struck a note or two as I dusted it. The mourning with the restraints and the ban on singing and playing had passed so quickly. I was sunk in gloom at the transience of things. My aunt, hearing the sound of the *koto*, sent over a poem from her apartments: "I hear the voice of a *koto* that has been silent, and my sadness breaks out afresh." Though there was nothing remarkable about the verse, I was deeply moved, and I answered: "'She will not return, though the day that stilled the *koto* has come again.'"

During the summer, it became clear that my sister,[95] who had been a source of strength to me for so long, was shortly to leave for the provinces. She postponed the trip until after the anniversary rites for my mother, but finally a day in the middle of the Ninth Month was set for her departure. It was a bitterly sad day for me. I went to see her off, taking along a set of robes and some trifles in a writing box as a parting gift, and found the place abustle with preparations. My sister and I were unable to look at each other; we were so overcome with tears that we drew harsh comments from onlookers. "Control yourselves, control yourselves," someone said, "this is hardly a lucky way to begin a trip."

I was wondering how I could possibly see her leave when a message came for me from the Prince: "I am at your house. Please hurry back." As my carriage was brought up, my sister and I took off our outer robes[96] and exchanged them as keepsakes; hers was light blue,[97] mine a thin russet-colored affair.[98]

The Prince scolded me for my inauspicious weeping, but I could not help myself. All the next day and on into the night, a beautiful moonlight night, I continued to think of her at the barrier[99] and beyond. My aunt too seemed deeply saddened. She was awake late playing her *koto* and sent over a poem: "My tears pour forth at the sound of this *koto*, and the suggestion of the ruined barrier that cannot detain her."[100]

I answered: "'My sleeves fade with the tears that wet them at the mention of that barrier.'"

And thus the year came to a close.

✳ *The Third Year of Kōhō (966)*

IN THE Third Month, the Prince was suddenly taken ill at my house. He was in considerable pain, and I was in great distress as I watched him and wondered what to do.

"I should like very much to stay here," he said, "but it would not be convenient for what must be done. I had best go home. Please do not think it cruel of me. Suddenly I feel even that I may not live much longer—it is most disturbing. Ah, if I do die, it will be sad to think how little I have left you to remember me by."

He was overcome with tears, and I grew quite dizzy with anguish.

"Do not cry," he began again. "It only adds to the pain. The saddest thing in the world, I think, is to have to leave someone when you are not ready for it. And what will you do? You cannot very well live alone, I suppose. But please, if you remarry, at least do not do it until after the mourning is over. Even if I live, I think I shall probably find it difficult to come here. While I am around, you can no doubt manage somehow. But if I am to die, there is nothing more I can do for you.'' He was in bed, speaking with difficulty and choked with tears.

Summoning my household, he continued : ''Do you know how I have felt about this lady? When I think that I may die without seeing her again, I find the prospect harder than I can tell you.'' Everyone was weeping by now, and I myself was speechless with tears. His pain was growing worse. His attendants helped him into his carriage, and he gazed at me as it pulled away and seemed genuinely sorry to leave. My own feelings I shall not attempt again to describe.

My brother, however, remained calm. ''What is all the wailing about? There is nothing really the matter with him. Let's hurry it up a bit.'' He climbed briskly into the carriage and escorted the Prince home.

Every day I wrote several letters to ask after the Prince. There may have been those who thought it unbecoming of me, but I could hardly worry about them, The replies, written by one of his oldest women attendants, consisted only of apologies for his inability to write himself. He was, I heard, considerably worse than when he left me. I was not able to look after him as I should have liked to, but I knew when he left that that would be the case, and there was of course no help for it.

More than ten days passed, and, with the proper prayers and rites, he began to improve a little. One evening[101] he wrote his own answer: ''This has been a strangely lingering illness; but I have been worried chiefly about the injury I may have done you.'' He had written in a very small hand, perhaps in a moment when no one was watching him. ''Since my mind is quite clear now,'' the letter continued, ''I should like to have you visit me some evening. To come openly would of course be out of the question, but it has been such a long time since I have seen you.''

I was worried about what people might think if such an expedition became known, but when he pressed me a second time to come, I decided I had to take the risk and asked for a carriage.

He had with some care prepared a room on an outlying corridor and lay waiting for me on the veranda.[102] I had the carriage light put out, and he seemed amused when I was unable to find my way in the darkness. He took my hand and guided me in.

"Why have you stayed away so long?" he asked, and we told each other of everything that had happened since our separation. Presently he called for a lamp. "It is really too dark—no, there is nothing to be shy about." He had it put behind a screen, from where it shed only a dim light.

He had not yet been allowed to eat fish, he said,[103] but he had had a meal prepared which, in honor of my coming, we might share. When we had eaten a little, the priests came in; it was getting late, and it was time for the curative spells and chants.[104] The Prince sent them away, however, saying he was somewhat better, and we were again left alone.

Toward morning I asked to have a servant called so that I might get away before daylight, but he pressed me to stay a little longer. It was still very dark, he said, and there was plenty of time. But even then it was getting lighter. He had the shutters raised, and as we looked out over the garden he asked me about my own. I was growing really alarmed at the lateness of the hour, but still he detained me. We would have some breakfast, he said. It was already broad daylight.

"Well, let me take you home, if you must go," he finally said. "I don't suppose you will want to come again."

"For me to have come at all," I protested, "will stir up I don't know what gossip, and it will only make things worse if you go with me. Please at least let me go alone."

"Well, if you must," he agreed. When the carriage came up, he arose and with considerable effort escorted me over to it. I was deeply moved.

"When will you be able to travel about?" I asked, and found the tears rising in my eyes.

"I am so very anxious to see you that I shall try somehow to visit you tomorrow or the next day," he replied, and he seemed truly grieved to see me go. The carriage was pulled away a little so that the ox could be hitched to it. He went back into the room, and, as we moved out the gate, I saw that he was still gazing in my direction. I found myself involuntarily looking back, and looking back again.

At about noon I had a letter, included in which was this poem: "Great was my grief when I thought we were parting forever; but still greater is my loneliness now that we have met again and parted again."

"I was much upset to see you in such pain," I answered. "'Our pleasant meeting was over too soon, and the way back was a trying one, beaten by waves of tears.'"

Two or three days later, although he was still far from well, he came to see me as he had promised. Gradually he recovered his strength, and his visits returned to normal.

At the Hollyhock Festival in the Fourth Month I recognized the carriage of a lady who had once been my rival, and I deliberately had my own carriage stopped beside it. While we were waiting, rather bored, for the procession to go by, I sent over the first line of a poem, attached to an orange and a hollyhock: "The hollyhock should promise a meeting, but the orange tells us we have yet to wait." After a time she sent back a line to complete the couplet: "Today for the first time I know the perverseness of her who sends this bitter yellow fruit." "'Why just today—she must have had similar feelings for years," said one of my women. When I told the Prince of the incident, he remarked, to our considerable amusement, that the closing line the lady really had in mind was probably more like this: "This fruit you send me, I would like to grind it to bits with my teeth."[105]

The preparations for the Iris Festival[106] this year were elaborate. I thought I would like somehow to see it, but there was no place reserved for me. Learning of my hopes, the Prince suggested that he might be able to arrange something, and when he invited me to a game of backgammon,[107] I insisted that if I won he should go ahead and look for reservations. Fortunately I did win. I happily began getting ready, and that evening when things were quiet I took out my brush and by way of practice jotted down a verse: "I count the irises over, but really I am waiting for the day when I can pull them up by the roots.''[108] He laughed and answered: "'They are hidden deep in the swamp; how can you be sure even that you have any irises?' ''[109]

But he did not want me to be disappointed, it seemed, and he found two places next to the Minister's stand and had them nicely appointed for the occasion.

He was kind enough in his way, and we had been together for more than ten years. Yet I could not but be conscious of my irregular position, and indeed I was aware of little else. I think that was not unnatural; on nights when the Prince did not come, we languished for want of company, and my father, really the only person on whom I could depend, had been away in the provinces now for more than ten years. Even on the few occasions when he was in the city, he was a good distance off, since his estate was in the Fourth or Fifth Ward and I was living beside the cavalry grounds in the First Ward.[110]

My house and garden were going to ruin. It apparently did not occur to the Prince how it hurt me to have him come and go without offering to help, indeed without seeming to notice that anything was wrong. He said he was busy, and perhaps he was; perhaps his duties outnumbered the weeds in my garden.

And so I looked out over the desolation, and the Eighth Month came. One day when we had been taking our ease rather pleasantly together, a series of trivialities led to strong words on both sides, and he left in a fit of rage. Calling our son out to the veranda, he announced that he did not intend to come again. The boy came back into the room weeping bitterly. He refused to answer my questions, but I knew very well what had happened, and, fearing the wild distortions my women might make of the affair, I stopped questioning him and tried instead to comfort him.

For an exceptionally long interval, five or six days, I had not even a note from the Prince. I was annoyed and bewildered. That he should have reacted so to what seemed to me no more than a joke indicated clearly the instability of our relationship. Indeed such a triviality might lead to a final break. As I was brooding over that possibility I came upon a bowl of water he had been using to dress his hair the day of the quarrel. It was covered over with a layer of dust, and illustrated with painful clearness the turn we had come to. A verse formed in my mind: "Has it all ended? Were there a reflection, I might ask it, but even the water-mirror he left has clouded over."

Eventually he appeared, but our interview was as unpleasant as before. There seemed no relief from the gloom that had become the dominant tone in my life.

In the Ninth Month, taking advantage of the autumn weather and scenery, I made a secret pilgrimage[111] to bring my situation to the attention of the gods. I left an offering of cloth with a poem attached at each of three branch shrines. First at the lower: "If their power extends even here to the base, let us have a favorable sign from the gods of this mountain." At the middle: "I look to these cedars for the profit of my trip, for a sign that my long years of prayer to Inari have been heard."[112] And at the upper: "I have climbed with great effort from god to god, but I do not think that my fortunes have climbed the heights with me."

Toward the end of the same month I went off quietly on another pilgrimage.[113] I left two offerings this time at each of the two shrines, and with them poems again. At the lower: "Is it dammed above or blocked below? This purification font, like my hopes, does not flow as well as it might." And, "Bark cloth tied firmly to sacred branch[114]— may the god not look upon me harshly." And at the upper: "When, when, I ask the dark groves of Kamo, will I come to a spot where the sun breaks through?" And, "Sleeves tied up by a cloth of bark;[115] if my unhappiness stops, I shall consider it a gift from these gods." But it was not a place where the gods were likely to hear.

Autumn passed and winter came, with its festivals and ceremonies, and high places and low hummed with excitement. But I spent my nights alone and my days in trivialities.

✻ *The Fourth Year of Kōhō (967)*

ONCE toward the end of the Third Month I happened to have some goose eggs, and, with nothing better to do, I thought it might be interesting to see whether I could string ten of them together; the old poem suggests what a difficult trick that is.[116] One after another I joined them, and then held them up in a strand—there they were, all ten of them. I thought this much too interesting to keep to myself, and sent the string off to the Imperial Consort from the Ninth Ward[117] with rather a commonplace note. "This is how you string ten eggs together," I remarked at the end of it. I received a poem in reply: "In comparison with my thoughts of you, these ten, remarkable though they may be, are a number hardly to be considered." And I answered: "'But what good are thoughts unrevealed? Let us exhibit them thus, time after time.'" I heard that she passed the eggs on to the Emperor's fifth son.[118]

On about the Tenth Day of the Fifth Month, the Emperor was taken ill. He died shortly after the Twentieth. The Crown Prince[119] immediately succeeded to the throne, and the Prince, my husband, who had been assistant chamberlain to the Crown Prince,[120] was made a first secretary in the Imperial Secretariat.[121] We should have been in mourning, but instead we were besieged with congratulations, and as I received all the well-wishers I found myself to an extent swept up in the triumph. Not that my real feelings had changed; it was only that crowds and activity had suddenly taken over my quiet life.

When I heard of the funeral preparations, I thought of those who had been near the late Emperor, and sent off several messages of condolence, among them this one to the Lady Jōganden (it was some days later):[122] "'Your heart must be away in the funeral mound, mourning the passage of the things of this world.'" "'I had not wanted to survive him,'" she replied "'and now my heart has gone off to the Mountain of Death.'"[123]

The forty-ninth-day rites[124] were conducted for the dead Emperor, and the Seventh Month came. Suddenly we heard that the Captain of the Guards,[125] though still young and apparently with no serious worries, had left his family and gone to Mt. Hiei to become a priest. Before we had recovered from the shock, we heard that his wife too had left the city and become a nun. I had occasionally corresponded with her, and I sent a poem of sympathy: "The thought of him in those deep mountains was sad enough—and now I hear that you are there too!"

Her reply came in the familiar hand: " 'I followed him to his hermitage, but I see that the rain clouds have come between us.' "[126]

The Prince was becoming rather a celebrated figure. There was much happy talk of promotions—to assistant chief of the Palace Guards, to the Third Rank, and the like.[127] But being always the center of attention made it difficult for him to visit me, he said, and in the Eleventh Month he moved me to a place near him where he could on occasion come without the bother of a carriage and retinue. And with that, one would think, my happiness should have been complete.

Toward the end of the Twelfth Month, the Lady Jōganden and her retinue moved into the west wing of my house. From before dark on New Year's Eve there was a great stir over the exorcism of devils.[128] I listened to it all happily.

✳ *The First Year of Anna (968)*

THEY had a quiet New Year's Day at the Lady Jōganden's, there being no gentlemen callers. I too had a quiet time, though I could hear a great commotion next door.[129] I thought of the poem about the thrush on New Year's Day,[130] and smiled over it as I listened.

One of my women, to while away the time, put legs on a pair of dried chestnuts, and loaded them on a little figure of a woodcutter. The doll had a swollen leg, and to that leg I pasted a poem written on a bit of colored paper: "A swollen leg must hurt like unrequited love, though of course we are not without the help of this staff."[131]

We sent it over to the Lady Jōganden, and presently it

came back, bits of dried seaweed twisted together on the end of the staff in place of the chestnuts, and a swelling even bigger than the first decorating the unswollen leg. With it was this poem: "When we compare, we find here a growth still larger, a yearning still more painful."[132]

Later in the day we exchanged festive dishes, and on the Fifteenth there were the usual observances.[133] In the Third Month, a letter apparently intended for the Lady Jōganden was delivered here: "I feel that I really must call on you, but I fear that 'another'—you will know whom I mean—would take it amiss."[134]

It was from someone very close to her, and someone in a position to tease her. I felt that I could hardly leave things as they were and passed the letter on after adding a poem in a very small hand: "The waves can hardly break over yon pine mountain—their own extravagant thoughts arouse them thus."[135]

Soon I received this acknowledgment: "'The waves are churned by the wind that beckons them to Matsushima; that explains their unruliness.'"[136]

Since she was acting as foster mother for the Crown Prince, she would shortly have to go back to court, and she had several times suggested that it would be unfortunate if she were to leave without having a good talk with me. One evening I visited her. Unfortunately just then the Prince came calling, and the voices of his party carried loudly across to the wing where we were talking. I ignored the disturbance.

"The poor fellow seems to be having trouble getting to sleep," she remarked after a messenger had come to summon me back. "He is likely to be difficult."

"But really he should be able to get along without a nurse-maid by now," I answered. I wanted to stay for a while at least, but more messengers came, and I had to leave. The next day, toward evening, the Lady Jōganden went back to court.

In the Fifth Month came the anniversary of the Emperor's death, and the Lady Jōganden again left court. She had planned to come here as before, but an unlucky dream forced her to go to the Prince's[137] instead. There the bad dreams continued, and one very bright night in the Seventh Month, as she was searching about for some way to avoid the bad luck they augured, she sent me this poem: "I know now how hard it is to seek through the sad autumn nights[138] an escape from the future a dream has told of."

I answered: " 'Sad indeed that must be; but just as sad to wait for a meeting that does not come.' "

And again from her: " 'I am seized, from a dream of a meeting, with a sadness and longing that lingers on.' "

And my reply: " 'But at least you have dreamed of a meeting; how is it when there is nothing, no word at all?' "

" 'No word at all'—what an unlucky thing to say," she came back in her next letter. " 'I see in a dream the one I would meet, but cannot cross over to that far bank; and must you add to my ill fortune?' "

And again I answered: " 'That river may keep two persons apart, but is it to separate their hearts?' "[139]

Thus we spent the night, passing notes back and forth.

I had wanted for some years to make a pilgrimage to the Hasedera,[140] and at about this time I tentatively decided on the Eighth Month. I was never free to follow my own inclinations, however, and I finally had to postpone it to the Ninth Month. The Prince pointed out that the purification for the *Daijōe*[141] was to be in the Tenth Month and that one of his daughters was to be the principal participant,[142] and he suggested that if I could wait until that was out of the way he might go with me. But the girl in question was no concern of mine, and I determined to start out as I had planned, quietly and without display. Since the omens for the first day were not good, we merely left the city and spent the night at the Hōshōji.[143]

Starting out again at dawn, we reached the Uji estate[144] by about noon. It was very quiet, and the surface of the river sparkled pleasantly through the trees. I thought how much noisier it would have been had anyone else been making the trip; I had decided, perhaps unwisely, to keep my retinue as small as possible. I had the carriage turned around and a screen of curtains spread, and, after my son had dismounted,

I raised the carriage blinds for a full view of the river. The fish traps[145] stretched away into the distance, and small boats dotted the surface, now passing up and down, now crossing one another in and out, more of them than I had ever seen before. My men, tired from the long walk, had found some odd-looking limes and pears and were eating them happily. It was most touching.

After lunch the carriage was loaded onto a ferry, and we crossed over and continued on, past Nieno Pond, across the Izumi River. The waterfowl moved me strangely. It was perhaps because I was traveling alone that I was so taken with everything along the way.

We spent the night at Hashidera. It was about six in the evening when we arrived, and a salad of chopped radish with some kind of sauce was brought out from what appeared to be the kitchen. Everything intensified the exciting awareness of being on the road. Even trivialities like this seemed quite unforgettable. In the morning we crossed another river, and the houses with their rough wattle fences made me think of something out of a romance, I could hardly say which one. We stopped at a temple again that night, and the following at Tsubaichi.

A heavy frost lay on the ground the next morning. Large numbers of people in travel costumes and leggings were passing by noisily on their way to and from the temple. In a room where the shutters had been raised, I waited for water to be heated, and as I looked out on the road I thought how each of these travelers must have his own problem, his own particular reason for making the pilgrimage.

While I was thus letting my thoughts wander, a person came with a letter from the Prince: "I have been rather upset these last two or three days. Are you quite all right, going off by yourself? And do you still intend, as you indicated, to spend three nights at the temple? If you can let me know when to expect you back, I shall somehow arrange to meet you."

"I have reached Tsubaichi," I answered, "and since I am this far I am thinking of going still deeper into the mountains. I therefore cannot give you a date for my return." But my attendants were upset at the idea of spending even three nights at the Hasedera, and the Prince's messenger heard of their misgivings before he went back.

There was nothing really spectacular about the way as we moved up toward the temple, but somehow I felt a sense of being deep in the mountains. The river roared and plunged along its rocky bed, and the leaves of the trees glowed through the banks of spray with varying suggestions of autumn color, deeply effective in the slanting light of the late-afternoon sun.[146] The road the day before had been uninteresting; it was still early for the autumn leaves, and the flowers had faded, leaving only the dry plumes of autumn grass. But here I was so moved that I raised the blind and drew aside the curtains for a better view. My clothes, rather wilted from the trip, seemed to have changed color.[147] As I took out a thin lavender train[148] and prepared to put it on, I noticed that here and there dead leaves had settled on it, and the lavender blended beautifully with their russet.[149]

The beggars at the temple, each with his earthen bowl, were most distressing. I recoiled involuntarily at being brought so near the defiling masses. I could not sleep,[150] and with little else to occupy my mind, I found myself fascinated, even moved to tears, at the prayer of a blind man, not very well dressed, who was pouring forth his petition in a loud voice without a thought that someone might be listening.

Though I really should have liked to stay longer, we started out with much of a stir the following morning. I had hoped to return as quietly as I had come, but I was besieged with invitations along the way, and in the end it turned out to be a rather noisy trip. At nightfall the third day, when we should have been back in the city,[151] we were only as far as Kuze no Miyake[152] in Yamashiro, and there was nothing to do but wait there for morning, wretched place though it was.

We started out again before daylight, and shortly we were overtaken by a man on horseback wearing a dark cloak. Some distance away he dismounted and got to his knees. "His Highness reached the Uji estate last night at about six o'clock,'' he reported, and we recognized him as one of the guards.[153] ''He ordered me to come ahead to inquire after Her Ladyship.'' My outrunners, excited at the news, prodded the ox-drivers on to greater speed.

As we approached the Uji River a fog closed in from behind, shutting off the road we had just come over. It was a gloomy morning. My carriage was stopped at the bank, and large numbers of men joined noisily in the process of unhitching it and loading it on a boat. The view over the river was strange and haunting, the fish traps just visible under the fog.

The Prince seemed to be waiting on the opposite bank, and I sent over a poem: ''A fickle one indeed: he comes now and then even to visit the fish in the traps at Uji.''

'' 'I have counted over the days to your return,' '' he answered, '' 'and on whose account have I come so far afield?' ''[154]

I continued to look out on the river while the carriage was being loaded, and presently we crossed over. Sons of fairly good families and certain junior officials,[155] I saw, were standing between the shafts of the carriage. The sun began to come through dimly, and here and there the fog gave way to blue sky.

The Prince, surrounded by numerous well-born attendants, among them the Captain of the Guards,[156] was waiting on the opposite bank. Like them, he was dressed for travel in a hunting robe.[157] We came in at a spot where the bank was exceptionally high, and it was with considerable difficulty that the carriage was hauled ashore.

We made it fast to a veranda, and, as we were eating a meal that had been prepared to break my pilgrim's diet,[158] someone remarked that the Lord Inspector,[159] who had an estate on the opposite bank, was in residence there to watch the fishing. We were certain that he would have heard of our being in the vicinity, and just as we had concluded that it would be wise to pay our respects a messenger approached with pheasants and fish tastefully attached to a branch of red leaves, and with them a letter from the Inspector: ''I have just heard that you are here and should like very much to see you, though I must apologize for being so unprepared.''

The Prince sent back that we had only just heard of the Inspector's being in the area, and that we should like to call immediately. He took off an under-robe and presented it as a reward to the messenger.[160] It appeared that adequate supplies, bass and carp and the like, had also been brought for the men, and the more pleasure-loving of them were soon drinking healthily. One, in a poetic flight, remarked on the singular way in which the sun struck the moons of the carriage wheels, and another decorated the rear shafts of my carriage with flowers and autumn leaves. ''We shall have at the same time blooming flowers and autumn fruits,'' he said happily.[161] My son thanked him for his trouble, and we crossed the river again, this time in two boats, the carriage propped up[162] facing the prows.

We picked to go with us the men we knew had a weakness for liquor, and somewhat later we turned back toward the city amid fuddlement and singing, and shouts of ''Hitch up her carriage, hitch it up there.'' But I was much too exhausted to enjoy the fun, and I found the trip back a trying one.

The preparations for the purification[163] were gaining momentum. The day after my return the Prince sent a list of chores for me to attend to, and, since there was little else to do, I hurried through them. Then came the purification itself, and the procession, the ceremonial carriages and all the attendants, men and women, a dazzling and stylish display; and after that a flurry of preparation for the inspection preliminary to the *Daijōe*.[164] I too was caught up in the general activity; and then came the end of the Eleventh Month, and another stir in preparation for the new year.

And so the months and the years have gone by, but little has turned out well for me. Each new year in turn has failed to bring happiness. Indeed, as I think of the unsatisfying events I have recorded here, I wonder whether I have been describing anything of substance. Call it, this journal of mine, a shimmering of the summer sky.

✳
✳ *Book Two*

✳ *The Second Year of Anna (969)*

THE OLD year passed as all the other years, and the new year came. It occurred to me that my unhappiness might be due to the fact that I did not observe fasts and penances as rigorously as most people. This year, I told my household, I would follow all the accepted prescriptions and see what would come of them.

My sister,[1] still in bed on New Year's morning, murmured something about a good-luck bag[2] into which we might put all our wishes. I would put him in too, I added—"That he may be with me thirty days and thirty nights a month."

My people were delighted. "Send that, just as you have said it, to the Prince—it should indeed bring good luck."

My sister got herself out of bed to join in the sport. "That should do better than any number of charms and oracles,"[3] she laughed.

I sent the message with my son. The Prince was a figure of considerable importance and his mansion was crowded with well-wishers. Though he was in a hurry to be off to court, he took time to write an answer. His reference was apparently to the fact that there was an intercalary Fifth Month[4] this year. "'Is it to take care of your excess love that we have had to put an extra month into the calendar?'"

I wondered if I had taken the joke a bit too far.

The next day my men were involved in a riot.[5] The Prince seemed sincerely sorry that the incident had occurred. I felt, however, that it was the unfortunate result of our living too close together. Presently I moved away. With great displays of pomp, the Prince would come to see me every other day or so. Things being as they were, such was, I suppose, the best that I could expect. Yet I found myself wanting to move back again—to go home, though not necessarily in brocade.[6]

The Festival of the Peach Blossoms came,[7] and we made all of the usual preparations. The retinue here being a modest one, however, the celebration was rather dull, and finally my people sent to the Prince's house inviting some of his attendants over: "'We must send to the estate of that peach fancier, Hsi Wang Mu,[8] for some really good revelers,'" they wrote.

The Prince's men came immediately, and with the festival offerings and all[9] there was much eating and drinking the rest of the day.

Toward the middle of the month, the men took sides for an archery meet, the sides practicing noisily on alternate days. One day the After Party[10] asked my ladies to offer rewards for the best scores. Nothing suitable was immediately to be had, however, and to gloss over the moment someone wrote this on a piece of blue paper and attached it to a willow branch: "'When the mountain wind first blows, it bends the shoots of the spring willows in the after direction.'"

There were all sorts of replies and replies to replies, but I have forgotten most of them. I shall leave it to the reader to imagine what their general quality must have been. One went this way: "'Since we do it with your support, we shoot with renewed vigor—like the willow buds opening in the spring.'"[11]

The meet was scheduled for the end of the month, but before it could be held a remarkable incident upset everything. I do not know what crimes they may have been guilty of, but a number of officials were demoted and banished, and finally, on the Twenty-fifth or Twenty-sixth, the Minister of the Left[12] too was dismissed from office. Great numbers of people crowded around his mansion in the western part of the city, but he fled without seeing them. They chased him off to Atago or Kiyomizu[13] or some such place and finally delivered a notice of banishment. It was all extremely sad, I thought, and when someone as distant as I from the event was so deeply affected there can hardly have been a dry sleeve in the city. His children were separated and sent off to remote provinces, who knows where, or forced to become priests—it was indeed unspeakably sad. The Minister himself became a priest, but they refused to respect his new status and bundled him off against his will to be Governor-General of Kyushu.[14]

This great incident drove everything else from our lives for the time. Though this is a journal in which I should set down only things that immediately concern me, the shock of the banishment was something very close to me, and I shall be forgiven, I hope, for treating it in such detail.

The first of the two Fifth Months[15] came, and toward the end of it the Prince was involved first in a penance and then in a long retreat at a mountain temple. I had word that he was suffering from the incessant rain, and I sent this note:
" 'An unfortunate time. The summer rains but grow louder, and the time you are away grows longer.' "

" 'If the rains and the days are only to increase,' " he sent back, " ' 'then would we not be happier getting wet together?' "

From about the end of the intercalary Fifth Month I was taken ill. It was nothing that could be specifically diagnosed, but I was in great discomfort. I cared little what happened to me and I did not want anyone, least of all the Prince, to think that I would have serious regrets at the thought of dying. My household nonetheless applied treatments feverishly, curative fires[16] and such, but nothing seemed to help.

The Prince, still in retreat, stayed away. He was building a new place.[17] On his way to and from overseeing the work he would sometimes stop by and inquire after me without presenting himself formally. One evening when I was in particular distress, he called and sent in a lotus pod from the new building; it was already dark, he said, and he would not disturb me. I sent back word that I was very ill, indeed barely alive.

I lay there thinking of this new place, how tasteful and well appointed it must be, and how he had indicated that he would take me to see it when it was finished. I did not know whether I would live or die, however, and I did not know how far his promise was to be trusted. My desire to see it, like most of my desires, might come to nothing. I murmured: "'Loves may bloom like the lotus and bear fruit, but I vanish from the world, a drop of dew on the floating lotus leaf.'"

The days went by and I felt no improvement. I thought it might be just as well if I were to die. I would have not the slightest regret for my life. But then I thought of what might happen to my son, and I was unable to hold back the tears.

Disturbed at my strangely lingering illness, my people called in a particularly virtuous and well-known priest, but his ministrations too had no effect. I began to feel that I would die; and if I were to die with so little warning, all the things I ought to and would like to have said to the Prince would have to go unsaid.

If only I could live until he came calling, I thought, I would be able, though perhaps not to say everything as I ought to, at least to leave some instructions and requests with him. But he did not come, and propping myself on an armrest with great difficulty I wrote him a letter:

"I want to say only that it seems I am to die. I had thought that we might have one more talk, but many evenings have gone by since last I saw you. I am strangely depressed. As I have frequently said, I have never expected to live long. My life itself is as unimportant as the dust, but I am extremely worried for the boy. He was most upset at your anger over that trifling business not long ago, and I hope that, unless you find him guilty of some really grave offense, you will be patient with him. My sins, I suppose, have been great. 'Perhaps the wind will blow in an unwished-for direction.'[18] If it does not the pains of this world will surely be felt by me in the next.' I shall be watching the two of you, and I shall know if you neglect him.

"You have chosen so far not to abandon us, in spite of indications that you might do so, and I hope now that you will watch after him. I have thought often enough that I should some day have to leave him to someone, and now it seems that that is indeed to be the case. I must ask your indulgence for the years before he is able to take care of him self. And perhaps I may hope also that you will not forget the secret words—the curious poems and such—that have gone between us. It is unfortunate that I have not found occasion to say these things directly to you. 'They tell us that the way of the dead is a steep and tearful one; but why are my sleeves so wet even here?' "

At the end I added, "Please remind him of my instructions that he is to be diligent in his studies," and on the outside I wrote, "To be read at the end of the mourning." I put it in a Chinese box[19] to which I was able to drag myself. My people may have thought it a strange performance, but if my illness was to be a long one I could find no peace without at least that out of the way.

The days went by with little change. The festival and purification of the Sixth Month[20] passed quietly, and finally toward the end of the month I began to feel somewhat more composed.

I heard about then that the Governor-General's wife[21] had become a nun. She had moved to her own mansion at Momozono[22]—her husband's was destroyed by fire three days after his banishment—and she seemed to be having a very lonely time of it there. My mind was not yet entirely clear (I was still in bed) and my thoughts on the incident accumulated in the wildest disorder, but still I tried to set them down in verse. It was rather a clumsy effort, I am afraid.[23]

> Thus have I thought, though to tell you now
> Can do no good, I suppose.
> The end of spring, a lament for the falling flowers,
> And then, like the song thrush singing its sweetest
>   burst
> And flying to the western hills, your lord
> Went off to that ominous mountain, Atago.
> Many were the voices raised in sympathy,
> The shocked and the grieved, and mine among them.
> Like a shy mountain stream that may hide in its valley
>   awhile,
> But must still come out, he was exiled far to the west.
> Our talk was of sorrow, and the *unohana*[24] came,

And the thrush gave way to the cuckoo, an unceasing
  lament
Sounding everywhere.
On into the rains of the Fifth Month, and where
In this gloomy world was one whose sleeves were dry?
And to one long month of rain was added another,[25]
Our sleeves so drenched that under and outer were
  merged,
Inseparable one from the other.
How much keener than ours is the grief of them
Whose sleeves are as the sleeves of farmers' muddy
  robes.
They are scattered to the four directions, only one
Is left in the nest, forlorn as the unhatched egg.
What shall we say of your lord himself,
In the realm of counties nine and islands two,
Where only a number recalls his far-off home,
The ninefold garlanded court?[26]
His wife left behind—is it but a dream, she asks.
When if ever will they meet again?
Lament upon lament, like the woodcutter's logs,
And tears like the salty brine from the saltmaker's
  sleeves.
A solitary nun, brooding and lonely
As a fisherman whose boat has gone adrift.[27]
Were it but for a time, a going and coming
As of the geese, the break would be less harsh.
But the dust collects where the pillow ought to be,
And where is one to look for the pillow itself?
Now, with the Rainless Month,[28] the tears are ex-
  hausted,
And the hollow cicada is left, its breast rent in two,
In the shade of the summer tree.
And when the autumn comes, and the dry reeds moan
About your fence in answer to the wind,
You will pass the long nights sleepless, no dreams of a
  meeting,
Your laments in tune with the wailing voices of insects,
Chanting the long night through.

I understand. I too am as the grass,
The dew-drenched grass in the grove of Oaraki.[29]
A sorrow such as yours, you may believe me,
I understand too well.

I added a short poem: "Who could have seen that your gate would be closed tight, blocked with weeds?"

My maids found the poem and urged me to send it to the Governor-General's wife. It was a fine expression of sympathy, they said. I finally agreed, but feeling that it would not be good to have her know who the author was, I had it rewritten on dark paper, folded it formally in an envelope, and fixed it to the end of a split stick. I instructed the messenger to say that it was from Tōnomine—her brother, the priest, was living there.[30] The messenger left immediately, before it could be passed into the house. I do not know what they thought of it.

Gradually I recovered my strength. On about the Twentieth of the Sixth Month the Prince set out for Mitake,[31] taking the boy with him. They left behind a suitable number of servants, and that evening I moved back to my old house, which had been fully repaired in my absence. I was greatly worried about the boy, but at dawn on the First of the Seventh Month the party came back safely. I was now a considerable distance from the Prince[32] and did not expect to see much of him; but at about noon on the day of his return he came by, fairly limping from the exhaustion of the trip. How is one to account for it?

Somehow the Governor-General's wife learned who had sent that poem. She got off an answer, but the messenger took it to the wrong house.[33] The people there sent an acknowledgment, I heard, though they must have found her letter a bit strange. The Governor-General's wife of course realized immediately that a mistake had been made. She was in something of a quandary: she could hardly send off the same letter again—we would surely know of it both here and at the other house and would think her rather a dunce, and she was not very proud of it in any case. Amused, I felt that I could not leave things as they were, and sent this poem to her, in the same hand as my earlier poem: "I hear the echo of an answer—but I know not where to seek for more." It was on light-blue paper, folded formally[34] and attached to a leafy branch.

The messenger again left without saying who had sent it, and, perhaps fearing a repetition of the earlier mistake, she delayed her answer for a time. She was of course quite justified if she thought my behavior odd. Finally, when she had a sure way of delivering it, she sent me this poem, written in a childish hand[35] on gray paper and attached to a juniper branch: "The wind rises. I think, 'Will not someone notice the smoke from the saltmaker's fire?' "[36]

I wrote my answer on walnut-colored paper and attached it to a sprig of withered pine: " 'I see the smoke rising from yon wild beach, but there is no wind to blow it my way.' "

In the Eighth Month there was a great stir over the fiftieth birthday of the Minister of the Left from Koichijō.[37] The Chief of the Left Guards[38] was preparing a congratulatory screen, and an emissary whom I could only with difficulty refuse pressed me to compose poems for the pictures scattered over it. I was not interested and tried several times to excuse myself.[39] But I could not escape, and one night, as I looked out at the moon, I wrote these verses down one and two at a time.

A congratulatory banquet is being held in someone's mansion:

"May this glad day long recur even as the sun and moon encircle the heavens."

A traveler has stopped his horse on the beach, and is listening to the sand plovers:

"At once we know—it is the call of the plover. May your years be as the number that call suggests."[40]

Horses are being herded past Awatayama.[41] The herdsman is resting in a house along the way and looking out at them:

"They have become friendly, through the long years, these ponies that pass by our mountain home."

Several ladies are looking at the full moon of the Eighth Month[42] reflected in a spring near a house, and on the avenue beyond the hedge[43] a man passes playing a flute:

"The voice of the bamboo flute beckons, and the auspicious moonlight seeps through the clouds."[44]

A pine grove stands in front of a farmhouse on a beach; some cranes are sporting under the trees (this picture, the instructions said, required two verses):[45]

"These little pines looking over the waves seem to pull at our hearts."

"O fortunate cranes, what worries could be weighing on *your* minds as you peer into the pine-shadowed sands?"

Fish traps have been set out:

"We go forth to watch the fish traps, and many enchanted nights we pass upon the road."

Fishing flares have been lighted along the beach, and fishing boats appear:

"We have come to a shore where life is worthwhile. Shine softly, you flares; move gently, you fishermen's boats."

A lady's carriage,[46] returned from gathering autumn leaves, approaches a house in an autumn grove:

"Those who live out their lives on the moor, one feels, look forward to autumn after autumn."[47]

Thus I wrote them down, but they seemed quite uninteresting. I heard, not without annoyance, that the poem about the flares and the poem about the cranes were the only ones used on the screen.

Autumn passed, and winter came, and events of little consequence[48] caused great commotions. A heavy snow fell in the Eleventh Month, and as I looked out I was for no particular reason filled with gloom, and with resentment at the Prince. "'The snow is as the accumulation of unhappy years,'" I wrote; "'the snow melts away, and I am not so favored.'"

* *The First Year of Tenroku (970)*

IN MID-SPRING the Prince's new place was finished. There was talk of his moving, now tomorrow, now today. He had evidently decided that I was to stay here. That decision came as no surprise. Indeed it seemed but natural, and, after the incident the year before, I was relieved to be at some distance from him.

In the middle of the Third Month an archery meet, a most elaborate one, was held at court. My son was chosen by the After Party,[49] and everything was dropped in the excitement of rehearsals, particularly for the dances to be presented by the winners. Everything else was put aside. The house echoed with music, even down to the steps prescribed for receiving prizes. I found it all most impressive.

On the Tenth the boy held a full rehearsal. Presents from the women's apartments and robes from the men were showered on O no Yoshimochi,[50] the dance master. The Prince was in penance and sent his apologies, but his attendants all came. In the evening, at the end of the rehearsal, Yoshimochi did a butterfly dance.[51] Someone gave him a yellow under-robe,[52] pleasantly in keeping with the season and the occasion, I thought.

On the Twelfth, the After Party planned a dress rehearsal. Since I had no archery range, they went to the Prince's. The junior officials[53] were there in force, I heard, and Yoshimochi was buried with congratulatory gifts. I wondered how the boy would acquit himself, but late that night he was escorted home in triumph by the Prince and a great many others. The Prince, apparently with no concern for the strange impression it would create, came in behind my screen after a time and told me of the day's events.

"The boy was most attractive and drew a great deal of praise," he said, "and his dance was extremely moving—everyone felt it. I have a couple of days of penance and won't be able to see to the preparations, but I shall come early on the morning of the meet to help him get ready."

And even I, despondent though I usually am, was swept up in the happiness of the occasion.

On the Fifteenth, the Prince came early as he had promised, and with him a great swarm of people to take care of the dancing robes and have last thoughts about the archery and all. Presently they went off with the boy and I spent the rest of the day wondering how everything would turn out. I was afraid all the toil over the dances would be wasted, for it was widely reported that the After Party had made an unfortunate choice of archers and was certain to lose.

The moon was bright that evening, and I left the shutters raised. Gradually they began to come back with reports of what had happened—he had shot so-and-so many points, and his opponent had been a certain captain of the Guards, and someone had failed badly, and someone else had shot well. I was by turns happy and sad. Finally it appeared that the After Party, doomed though it had been to defeat by all the prophets, had scored a series of hits and earned a draw.[54]

My nephew[55]—he was about the same age as my son—danced in celebration a masked pantomime about a Chinese warrior.[56] They had taken turns practicing their dances at my house and his. The boy danced next and made a remarkably good impression, I was told. He was given a robe by the Emperor.[57]

Presently the boy came home, riding with the ''Chinese warrior'' and escorted by the Prince. The Prince was most enthusiastic. The event had added much to his prestige, he repeated over and over again with great emotion, and all of the great figures[58] present had been stirred by the boy's performance. He called in the archery tutor and loaded him with presents, and I forgot my unhappiness for a time in the general triumph. That evening and for the next two or three days, everyone I knew, priests even, called and sent messengers to offer congratulations.

From about the Tenth of the Fourth Month to the Tenth of the Fifth the Prince was ill. I saw nothing of him, though there was a message. For seven or eight days he had been confined at the Minister's,[59] he said, amid priests and exorcists. He had hoped to risk a visit here late some night; but it would not do to have word get out, since he was absent from court on grounds of illness. The messenger said that he seemed well enough, and I waited in vain for a visit.

I was puzzled. Each night I secretly expected to see him, but finally even his letters stopped, and there followed a long period of complete silence. In spite of my bewilderment, I tried to pretend that I noticed nothing amiss. At night I would lie tense at the sound of the carriages passing by, and then I would somehow drift off to sleep and wake to another joyless morning. The boy frequently saw his father, but there seemed to be no definite reason, nothing one could really strike at, for his coolness. Nothing in fact came of the interviews, and the Prince did not even ask after my health. And surely it was impossible for me to take the initiative and ask him what had caused this strange aloofness.

One morning after the shutters had been raised, I looked out and saw that it had rained during the night, and the trees were covered with dewlike drops. I jotted down a verse: "A dew has fallen on the leaves while I have waited through the night; the dew will vanish with the sunlight, but the waiting must still go on."

The Great Minister of State[60] died toward the end of the Fifth Month. The Prince sent word that, with the succession and all so uncertain, it would be best for him to keep out of sight. He also sent some mourning robes for me to put together, but in view of his recent behavior, I saw no reason why I should be expected to serve him, and I sent them back with the excuse that the lady who took care of such things was unfortunately away visiting her family. This may have annoyed him more than usual. I heard not a word from him.

The Sixth Month came, and counting back I found that he had not visited me in the evening for more than thirty days, and in the daytime for more than forty. It would be a great understatement to say that I found this sudden turn of events strange. Our relationship had never been a satisfactory one, but still this was the first time that such a long and complete separation had occurred, and even my attendants found it bewildering. I could not keep my mind fixed on anything, but would spend my time gazing listlessly at the garden, or, ashamed to have anyone see me, lie with my face pressed against the floor to hide my tears. Once, although its season was past, I heard the call of a song thrush, and a verse formed in my mind: "Do you too have some limitless sorrow, O song thrush, that you cry thus on into the Rainless Month?"[61]

I grew increasingly restless toward the end of the month, and, tormented by the hot weather, I decided to go to Karasaki[62] on the lake shore for the purification,[63] and in the process possibly to find some peace of mind and a refuge from the heat. I set out with the boy,[64] a friend in much the same situation as myself,[65] and seven or eight outriders. The moon was bright, and dawn was just beginning to break in the east as we crossed the river. Presently the road turned into the mountains. It was as though we were cleanly shut off from the city, and I felt a strong sense of release, a reaction no doubt from the depression that had been plaguing me so. At the barrier[66] we stopped to rest and feed the animals. Some woodcutters came pulling their carts down from the dark woods above, so new a sight to me that it was almost as if I had been reborn into a different world.

I was taut with emotion as we rode down from the barrier. The vista stretched on into the distance, endlessly it seemed. As I stared at what I first took to be a couple of birds, I saw that they were fishing boats on the lake. Dulled though my emotions had become, I was moved to tears by the beauty of the scene, and my companion even more strongly. We were quite unable to look at each other.

With still a great distance ahead of us we reached Otsu, a collection of untidy huts. Wretched indeed they were, but to me everything was interesting. We passed through the town and came out on the lake shore, and behind us along the beach were clusters of houses with rows of boats moored before them. On the lake other boats moved in and out, cutting across and back one in front of another.

Toward noon we pulled up under the lone sandalwood tree[67] that had announced Shimizu from some distance away. We still had a long road before us, and we decided to rest until lunch was brought up. The carriages were unhitched, the animals were cooled along the beach, and my son, leaning against the tree as though thoroughly exhausted, helped himself from a bag of sweets. Presently lunch came, and after we had divided it half the outriders started back for the city to report that we had come safely thus far.[68]

After a time we rehitched the carriages and headed in the direction of the shrine.[69] A high wind had come up, and a heavy surf beat in on the shore as we cut among the small boats being pulled in.

At the urging of my men, certain fishermen on the beach struck up a song, in indescribably resonant voices. We finally arrived at Karasaki, but we had scarcely enough energy left for the services.

The shrine was on a narrow promontory, so narrow that the lower carriages[70] were practically in the water. As we climbed out, the waves did indeed, after the old proverb, seem to sweep everything before them.[71] The people in the rear carriages[72] seemed on the verge of falling out in their curiosity—they exposed themselves quite to the public view[73] as they fluttered and cried out over the exotic ritual offerings.[74] Meanwhile the young men of my escort were lined up some distance away singing most effectively the shrine song, "Karasaki in Shiga."[75]

The wind was strong, but with no shade it was extremely hot. Toward the middle of the afternoon we started back, rather in a hurry to reach Shimizu. As we passed along the coast I found myself reluctant to leave it behind; but there was no stopping, and late in the afternoon we started up the pass. The evening cicadas[76] were at their peak. I composed a poem all for myself—I told it to no one:

> And is there someone, noisy singers at the gate,
>
> Outsinging one another—someone you await?

Toward Hashirii the outriders speeded up their horses, and several of them reached Shimizu considerably ahead of us and looked enviably cool when we arrived. They approached in high spirits to unhitch the carriages.

My companion began a verse: "One envies the horses whose steps grow quicker as they approach this Hashirii."

And I finished: "The shadow passes swiftly over the cool waters of Shimizu."[77]

We had the carriages drawn in near the water at the upper end of the station and climbed out behind a screen of curtains. I found myself relaxing into a pleasant calm as I washed my hands and feet in the cool water. We ate sitting on rocks, with the dishes on the water troughs, and prepared our own rice—such a rare delight of a picnic that I hated the thought of leaving. But already it was getting late and the men were nervous, and as the sun went down we reluctantly started off. I had thought that here at least nothing could happen to upset me.

At Awata a messenger from the city met us with a torch. The Prince, he said, had called that day. I was astonished—he must have deliberately chosen a day when he knew I would not be home. My attendants questioned the messenger about the visit, and so I reached home, the happiness of the day turned to utter dejection. He had called and been told exactly where I had gone, my people said, and he had expressed his disappointment. I listened in a daze.

The following day we spent recovering from the trip, and the day after that the boy called on his father. I was reluctant to ask about that extraordinary visit, but memories of the pleasant day on the lake shore got the better of me, and I sent along this verse, with instructions that the boy was to deliver it and leave before his father had a chance to read it: "I thought I had wept my share of tears in this sad world; but along that shore they came welling back, a keepsake, it seemed, from earlier days."

I waited for some indication that he had read the poem and understood, but he was silent for the rest of the month. Some time before, when I had been overseeing the garden, I had found some rice shoots and had them gathered and planted in under the eaves. I had had them carefully watered and had watched them swell into the beginnings of grain heads; but just as the leaves were turning gold they withered and died. "'Under these sad eaves, where the life-giving lightning[78] fails to reach,'" I wrote, "'the young grain too seems to retreat into its thoughts.'"

The Lady Jōganden[79] had two years before become a Mistress of the Palace Women's Quarters.[80] It seemed odd that she had never sent a word of sympathy to me in my domestic difficulties, and I thought perhaps she might be keeping aloof because of family quarrels.[81] Then it occurred to me that she might not have heard of my estrangement from the Prince, and I sent her a letter and a poem: "The spider continues to work at his thread even when it seems certain to break; and shall we be less diligent with the thread between us?'' She sent a long and friendly answer, including a poem: ''How sad to hear it is broken—though not a spider's, it is a thread into which long years have gone.'' It appeared that she had known all along and had deliberately kept her silence.

I was rather hurt, and while I was thinking the matter over, a note came from the Prince: ''You have not answered my letters, and your lack of affection has forced me to keep my distance. I do plan to come today, however.''

I set about a reply, upon the urgings of my attendants, but it was evening before I had it finished, and he appeared before the messenger could possibly have reached his mansion. My people, suspecting that he was up to something, urged me to pretend that nothing was wrong and see how he behaved. Somehow I controlled myself and received him.

''I have had quite a string of penances lately,'' he said, ''and that has kept me away. I have certainly never considered leaving you, but I have been somewhat upset by your jealousy.'' Thus again he put on a mask of frankness and good will, and I was all the more unconvinced.

Early the next morning he left. He had work to do, he said, but he would come again in a day or two. I did not really believe him. Still I thought he might have had a change of heart[82]—and then in the back of my mind was always a fear that he might not come again. The days went by and that fear seemed to have some substance. His offhand promise had only made my uncertainty the more painful. I was obsessed with thoughts of death and suicide, but concern for the boy restrained me. If only I could get him properly reared and married to some nice reliable woman, I thought, I would feel easier. But then I thought of how helpless he would be without me, and the idea of dying became a painful one.

Once, to see how he would react, I suggested to the boy that I might retire and become a nun. Child though he was, he burst into tears. ''If you do that, I will become a priest,'' he said. ''What reason would there be for me to go on as I am?''

I too was seized with an uncontrollable fit of weeping, but I tried to make a joke of the whole thing. "And when you have become a priest," I said, "will you still keep your hawk?"

He promptly got up, went over to where the hawk was tethered, and released it. My ladies were all in tears, and I of course was still more deeply touched. "'If, with these quarrels, I must become a nun,'" I said to myself, "'the first sorrow is for the vanished hawk.'"[83]

That evening a letter came from the Prince. It seemed to me utterly insincere, and I dismissed the messenger without an answer. I was not feeling well, I said.

The Festival of the Dead[84] came, with the usual excitement, in the middle of the Seventh Month. The Prince had always been careful to send supplies for the occasion, but this year I thought we had perhaps grown too far apart. I wondered whether my dead mother too would be made unhappy by the oversight. Still I did not give up hope, and I determined to wait, before I prepared offerings myself, to see definitely whether he intended to ignore me. I shed many tears of apprehension, but presently a letter came and the usual packages. "You have not forgotten my dead mother," I answered, "but I, like Tsurayuki, must continue to languish, unable to renounce the world as I should like to."[85]

And still his behavior was odd. He could hardly have found another lady friend, I thought—and I began to wonder. One of my women remarked that he seemed interested in an attendant of the late Regent,[86] the one called Omi.

"Oh, her!" someone said. "She is quite the sport, I hear. Maybe he has stopped coming here because he wants her to think he has cleared up his other affairs."

"Hardly," the first replied. "She is almost too good-natured and should be easy enough to win. I don't think he would have had to go to all that trouble."

"Then there is that daughter of the old Emperor.[87] Could anything be going on there?"

"Well, he is after someone, we can be fairly sure of that," they concluded. "But in any case you will not accomplish much sitting here moping, as cheerful as the last light of day. Why don't you make a pilgrimage somewhere?''

Indeed I had nothing to do but sit and brood. Yet it was so extremely hot—but then, as they said, there was nothing to be gained by staying on here. So, in the middle of the Seventh Month, I decided without consulting anyone to go to Ishiyama.[88]

I started out quietly before daybreak, not even telling my sister. Somehow they heard about it back at the house, and at the river I was overtaken by a few attendants.[89] The sky was bright with the late moon, the way was quiet, and we met no one. There was a dead body lying in the river bottom as we passed, but I was quite beyond being frightened by that sort of thing.

At Awatayama[90] we stopped to rest. I was feeling utterly wretched. My thoughts were out of control, and I could not hold back my tears. But it would not do for anyone to see me, and with an effort I pulled myself together and we started off again.

By the time we reached Yamashina the sun was high. I felt completely naked and exposed in the bright daylight, and my thoughts were in such chaos that I feared even my basic sanity might be swept away. I put my attendants out some distance in front and behind to avoid the appearance of a retinue and walked quietly by myself. Even so the sight must have puzzled those who passed us, and I was keenly conscious of their whispered remarks. Yet somehow I forced myself on.

At Hashirii we stopped to eat. As we were spreading the screens and getting things ready, a terrific shouting came up from the east. Who could it be, I wondered. Surely someone in the party would recognize my attendants—what a wretched stroke of luck! On they came, a considerable number of mounted outriders, and then, with great ostentation, two or three carriages. It was, I was told, the Governor of Wakasa[91] and his family on their way back to the capital. Fortunately they went by without stopping. There they were, taking complete advantage of their rank, without a cause for complaint. They were the sort of people who, when they were in the city, had to go about on their knees, but here on the road see how they enjoyed themselves. I was more conscious than ever of my own unhappiness.

Some of the outriders and attendants came up near my screens and proceeded noisily to wash themselves in the stream. Their deportment was quite scandalous. My men could only tell them to go away, but they were incensed: "This is a public highway, isn't it? Who do you think you are, ordering people around like that?" But finally we saw them off and started out again over the pass.

I was completely exhausted when we reached Uchideno-hama, and in a daze climbed into a boat my outrunners had equipped with mats and awnings. The loneliness, the pain, the sorrow I felt as we set off down the river can surely have had few parallels.[92]

Late in the afternoon we reached the temple. I washed myself in the purification hall and tried to rest, but I could only toss and weep.[93] I washed myself once more and went up to the main hall. I could not control my sobs long enough to tell my story to the Buddha, however, and, choked with tears, I looked out into the night. The hall was built high over a heavily wooded valley,[94] and the moon, just past full, here and there leaked through the trees, lighting the river down which we had come. The spring at the foot of the hill shone like a mirror.

I had been leaning on the banister and gazing out for some time when I heard a rustling and a strange cry on the hillside. It was a deer, I was told, and as I was wondering why it did not sound as a deer ought to, I heard a young, vibrant answering call from farther off in the valley. The sound of it echoed on in the night, so lonely, so penetrating, that I was quite driven from my meditations.

For a time I was able to concentrate on them again. Then I was startled by the raucous shout of a farmer guarding his fields somewhere beyond the hill. Thus everything conspired to break the harmony of my thoughts. I went through the pre-dawn prayers[95] and retired exhausted to the purification hall.

A gentle wind was blowing, and a mist drifted in from the east as the dawn grew brighter. In the distance, beyond the river, untethered ponies were foraging about—it was all like a picture. And then suddenly I thought of my son, whom I had left behind lest I attract too much attention. And I thought of how I should like to die, and only this one bond with the world restrained me.

Some of my men wanted to go to Sakunadani, which was not far away, but another warned that it was rather a dangerous place—people were always being caught in the current. I thought myself that I would not mind that fate at all.

I had quite lost my appetite, and when I heard that there was *shibuki*[96] growing in the pond behind the temple I had it brought in and ate it with a sauce and chopped limes,[97] a most interesting dish.

I spent that night too at the main hall, weeping and praying. Toward dawn I dozed off and dreamed that a priest, the manager of the temple's affairs, it appeared, came up with a pitcher of water and poured it on my right knee. I awoke with a start. It must have been a sign from the Buddha, an unhappy one, no doubt.[98]

Someone came to tell me it was nearly dawn, and shortly afterward we descended from the temple. It was still quite dark, but the surface of the water glowed white in the distance. Though I have spoken of how few attendants I had, there were in fact some twenty of them, and, as I looked down at the boat moored to the bank, I thought it seemed a bit small for such a large party.[99]

The priest who had lighted the votive lights for me was at the bank to say good-by, a sad expression on his face. It occurred to me that it would hardly be pleasant to stay on year after year in this temple, familiar to the point of boredom.

My men promised to bring me back the following year. "Please do," he said, and he continued to stand there, a lonely shadow in the dawn, as we rowed off.

The moon had grown pale and was reflected in pinpoints on the surface of the water as the wind stirred the waves. "Your face has grown thin,"[100] my men sang in faint, sad voices, and I felt the tears come to my eyes. As we rowed through the rushes past Ikagasaki and Yamabukinosaki, we heard a splashing and a melancholy song in the distance, and presently we made out an approaching boat. It was headed for Ishiyama, we were told, to meet someone. Obviously this was ours arriving late, and we had one that had been in Ishiyama all along. Some of the men jumped over, and off they rowed up the river, singing quite without restraint. It began to grow lighter as we passed under the Seta Bridge,[101] and we could see the sand plovers flying in and out along the bank. Everything was strangely moving in the gray dawn.

At Uchidenohama a carriage was waiting, and we reached the city shortly before noon. "You caused quite a stir," my people said. "We wondered whether you might have done something rash, maybe gone off for good this time."

"Let them think what they like," I answered. "And am I still enough of a person to cause a stir?"

Shortly afterwards came the wrestling meet at court.[102] The boy indicated that he would like to go, and I sent him off properly equipped. He first stopped by to pay his respects to his father, and the two of them went on together. In the evening he came back escorted by some underling, when the Prince of course should have come himself. I was much chagrined to hear that he had business "elsewhere."

The boy went to the tournament again the following day, but his father paid little attention to him and sent him back in the evening with some minor officials from the Secretariat.[103] He himself left early, I was told. It was a departure from good form that must have hurt the boy deeply, and I myself felt cut to the very heart as I saw him come in lonely and dejected.

On the Second of the Eighth Month, late in the evening, the Prince suddenly appeared. His behavior was extraordinary. "Lock all the doors," he demanded. "Tomorrow we are in penance."

I was furious. My people gathered about and listened, and in their consternation could only imitate me, and whisper to one another that we must be calm. I was left to sit with him, and no doubt I looked spiritless and foolish.[104]

The Prince and I talked together all the next day, but his conversation was only a series of variations on the same theme: "I have not changed. Why will you look at everything in the wrong light?" I shall not go into my answers.

On the autumn lists, published the Fifth, he was duly promoted to General of the Guards,[105] and the rejoicing was loud. After that I saw him rather more often. He suggested that during the celebrations in the fall for the *Daijōe*[106] he would ask the ex-Emperor to give the boy an official rank,[107] and in preparation set the coming-of-age ceremony for the Tenth of the month. Everything went off as it should, with the Genji Dainagon[108] bestowing the court headdress. My direction was banned by the oracles for that day, but the Prince, excusing himself on the grounds that it had grown very late, stayed the night anyway.[109] He was most kind; still I could not but wonder whether, now that the boy had officially reached maturity, this was not the last time I was to be so honored.

His visits in the Ninth and Tenth Months were infrequent.[110]

There came the excitement of the *Daijōe* purification. We had stands, somewhat nearer the royal chair than I would have wished. The spectacle was dazzling indeed. "But she is not the inferior of anyone in sight," I heard people say. "What a shame he does not realize it."[111] I was most immoderately flustered.

The Eleventh Month came and the preparations for the *Daijōe* were noisy and obtrusive. The Prince, apparently afraid that the boy might be inadequately prepared for receiving his rank, came oftener than usual,[112] and urged us to take special pains with the lessons. Indeed we were all rather nervous and upset. Early on the night of the *Daijōe* he came to see me. He should, he said, have accompanied the Emperor back to the palace, but that would have made him extremely late, and, pleading an illness, he had come away here instead. What might people think? Be that as it might, he wanted to see that the boy was properly garbed and would escort him to the palace the next day.[113] It was a little as though the pleasant old days had come back.

Since his retinue had not come, he went off the next morning to see to it, leaving instructions that the boy, properly accoutred, was to follow. They made a series of courtesy calls, it seemed, and I was most touched and pleased.

Thereafter I was in penance. On the Twenty-second I had a note which implied that I was only making excuses, and that I might expect to see him. Late in the evening, however, the boy came home and reported that his father had gone elsewhere. If things had been as they once were, I thought, he would surely have come on such an occasion.

For a couple of weeks I heard nothing. On about the Seventh of the Twelfth Month he stopped by before dark, but I did not feel up to a direct interview and received him from behind a curtain. Seeing how matters were, he presently left. It was getting on toward evening, he said, and he had had a summons from the palace. And again for some ten days I heard nothing.

One day, as I sat looking out at the rain, knowing that today there was less chance than usual of seeing him, my thoughts turned to the past. The fault was not mine, there was something wanting in him. It had seemed once that wind and rain could not keep him away. Yet, thinking back, I saw that I had never been really calm and sure of myself. Perhaps, then, the fault was in fact mine: I had expected too much. Ah, how unwise it had been to hope for what was not in the nature of things.

The rain continued on into the evening. I heard someone going into the south apartment,[114] a suitor no doubt. Feigning a calm which I did not feel, I remarked to an old attendant that it was indeed gallant of him to come out on such a bad night.

"Yes," she replied, "but the Prince used to come on worse nights than this."

At that I quite lost control of myself. A poem formed in my mind which I repeated over and over until dawn: "I try to keep back these memories; but with the flame in my heart the tears boil over."

I did not try to sleep that night.

I saw him but that once during the Twelfth Month. The year-end ceremonies were of the usual sort, and I shall not stop to describe them.

✳ *The Second Year of Tenroku (971)*

HE HAD always visited me on New Year's Day, and this year too he would surely come, I thought. At about two in the afternoon there was a great shouting as his outrunners cleared the way, and my people bustled about getting ready to receive him. But he went on. He is in a hurry, I thought, and will perhaps be back later. But night came, and we saw nothing of him.

Early the next morning he sent a servant to pick up some robes he had asked us to sew, and incidentally to deliver a message : ''I went past your gate yesterday thinking to stop by later, but somehow the day was over before I got around to it.''

I wanted to ignore him, but my women persuaded me that it would be unlucky to start out the new year in anger. Finally I sent off a note, rather a nasty one. I was most unhappy at the time because I had become convinced, and indeed it was much talked of abroad, that he was carrying on with that woman Omi.[115]

Late on the afternoon of the Third there was a shouting that even outdid the earlier one. My people again rushed out to welcome him, opening the inner gate and kneeling in readiness for his arrival. I felt only that their efforts would be wasted, that the incident of New Year's Day would be repeated. Still I waited with repressed excitement. He drew near and passed on. I may perhaps leave it to the reader to imagine how I felt.

The following day there was a New Year banquet at a mansion near mine. I kept my hopes to myself, but I thought perhaps, even though I had not heard from him, he might stop by. I hung desperately on the sound of each carriage as it drew up, and then, late in the evening, listened tensely for each approaching outrunner as the guests left for home.

They passed my gate, and I held my breath, and then there were no more. Sleepless I waited for the dawn.

Early one morning I received a note. Evidently he felt that he had to write a note now and then. I did not answer. A couple of days later came another: "I know I have neglected you, but I have been extremely busy. Would it be convenient if I were to come tonight? I am somewhat apprehensive about how I will be received."

I sent back word that I was not feeling well and could not answer. I was sure that I would not see him, but presently he appeared, cool and nonchalant as ever. His playful manner I found most irritating, and before I knew it I had begun pouring out all the resentment I had stored up through the months. He said not a word, pretending to be asleep, and after I had gone on for a time he started up and exclaimed, "What's this? Have you gone to bed already?"

It may not have been entirely gracious of me, but I behaved like a stone for the rest of the night, and he left early in the morning without a word.

He continued to pretend that nothing was amiss and sent laundry and sewing for me to take care of, but I sent it back undone. For more than twenty days I heard nothing from him. Spring came, and the song of the thrush, and I murmured over to myself some words from an old poem: "Spring renews everything, and only I grow old."[116]

Around the middle of the Second Month there was a widely circulated rumor that he had spent ten days running with his newest lady friend.

Higan Week[117] came, and I prepared to go into a retreat—it seemed at least a fair alternative to this constant brooding and weeping. The quilts were taken up for plain clean mats,[118] and the house cleaning stirred up great clouds of dust. As I watched it all, I thought how unprepared I had been for these misfortunes.[119] " 'My sorrows outnumber the specks of dust as we gather up these quilts.' "

I thought too that I should like to go on a long retreat at some mountain temple. Such a retreat might make it easier for me ultimately to renounce the world. My people argued that autumn retreats were really more beneficial,[120] and then too my sister[121] was having a child and I could not very well leave her at such a time. I decided, however, to go away during the Fourth Month.[122]

I became preoccupied with the idea of the worthlessness of material things, and when someone offered to send me some bamboo that I had asked for the year before I tried to refuse it. "I do not feel that I am long for this world," I said, "and I no longer concern myself with worldly things."

"But this is most narrow of you," my friend replied. "Remember Gyōgi Bosatsu[123]—he planted a fruit orchard for those who would survive him."

That seemed a reasonable view. I asked to have the bamboo sent over, and I wept as I planted it, thinking that perhaps someone years after might see it and remember my life in this sad place.

Two days later came a heavy rain and a driving wind from the east, and some of the new bamboo was knocked over. The rain did not stop long enough for us to go out and reset it. "'The bamboo has been blown in unexpected direction,'" I recited, "'and so it is with us as we come to the end of this weary life.'"[124]

All through the Twenty-fourth a gentle rain was falling. Toward evening I had an odd letter from him: "I have been put off by your fearsome antics and have stayed away these many days." I did not answer.

The rain continued the following day, but my tears proposed to outlast it. As I sat looking out I thought of the poem about retreating from the world when the joy of spring is at its height.[125] "These thoughts torment me in infinite detail," I recited to myself, "and my tears fall as the drops of rain."

Toward the end of the Third Month I prepared to move to my father's house, both because the horoscope demanded it[126] and because I felt the need of something to break the monotony. Since my sister's child had been born safely, I made arrangements too for the long retreat, and into this twofold confusion came a letter from the Prince: "Perhaps I may hope that you have by now un-disinherited me. If you will allow it, I may come this evening."

I was in no mood to answer, but my women insisted that
to ignore him would be rude and could only lead to further
unfaithfulness. I finally sent back one sentence: "After you
have let so many moons pass unnoticed, it would be strange
for you to turn up now when there is no moon."

I thought surely he would not come, and went hastily
ahead with the move to my father's. But he appeared, late
in the evening, quite as if he had seen me but that afternoon.
He annoyed me as much as ever. In that small house, however, so crowded with servants, it was impossible to express
my resentment. Indeed I felt that I could hardly breathe, and
I spent the night with my hand against my breast.

Early the next morning he left. Again he had "all sorts of
business to attend to." Perhaps it was so, and I might better
have let the matter rest;[127] but I waited expectantly night
after night for some word from him. The end of the month
came, and I heard nothing.[128]

. . . His place was very near. My people only upset me by
saying, "There is a carriage in front of his gate. Maybe he is
coming here." And those who tried make me answer his letters I found equally trying. Indeed I was more distressed than
ever.

On the First of the Fourth Month I called in the boy. "I
am beginning a long retreat," I explained, "and it is said
that you are to be with me."

I made no elaborate preparations, simply put some incense in an earthen dish on my armrest and began praying
and meditating. "I have never really been happy," I thought,
and the tears began, "and now things are worse than ever.
If only the Buddha would let me be reborn in enlighten-
ment." I remembered how once, when someone had remarked on the incessant fingering of rosaries and reading of
sutras that had become fashionable, I had retorted that praying women were worse than nuns and would surely be
widows before long. And now where had my cynical ideas
gone? Day and night I was busy with prayers, somewhat
listlessly and aimlessly, perhaps, but almost without pause.
Those who had heard what I said then must certainly be
smiling now. My marriage being the uncertain thing it was,

what could have prompted that unfortunate display of wit?

I wept on. Embarrassed to be seen in such a condition, however, I concealed my tears as best I could.

On about the twentieth day of the retreat I dreamed that my hair was cut and my forehead bared like a nun. Seven or eight days later I dreamed that a viper was crawling among my entrails and gnawing at my liver, and that the proper remedy for the difficulty was to pour water over my face. I do not know whether these dreams were good or bad, but I write them down so that those who hear of my fate will know what trust to put in dreams and signs from the Buddha.

Early in the Fifth Month I had a note from the people at my house asking whether they should put out irises[129] even though I was not at home. Not to do so, they thought, might be bad luck. I wondered what difference it could possibly make and jotted down a verse: "I have grown away from the world—what have these irises to do with me?" I wanted to send it to them, but I knew that they would not understand.

After the retreat I went home again. The rainy season had begun, and the monotony was more oppressive than ever. In the intervals between prayers I had the flowers and grasses in the garden dug up and separated. They had spread in the rankest profusion during my absence.

That gaudy procession went by once more. There was a great clamor as it approached my gate. I was just going through my prayers. Again my people got ready for him, and again I waited tensely, expecting the worst. And the procession moved off without even a nod for us. My people stared dumbly at one another, and I was unable to collect myself for the better part of the day.

"What can he be thinking of?" someone remarked tearfully.

"It is indeed unfortunate," I answered, with an effort at composure. "I have been subjected to this because I have allowed myself to be kept here. I should have gone away as I wanted to long ago." My anger and chagrin quite passed description.

At the beginning of the Sixth Month I was surprised by a

letter from him. He was in penance, the messenger said, and the letter had been pushed out from under his gate.[130] "You should have finished your retreat by now," he wrote. "Why are you still hiding away there? It is so inconvenient that I have not been able to visit you. And then I have had this de-filement, and I have had to forego pilgrimages and such."

Surely he should have known that I was back, I thought in some annoyance. I controlled myself and prepared an an-swer: "Such a strange letter—where might it be from, I wondered. I have been back for some time, but you could of course have no way of knowing. You are going these days, I am told, to places where you would be unlikely to hear. I really should have gone away for good long before this, how-ever, and I make no complaints."

It had become painful even to get these rare letters, these little flashes into the past, and I was sure, moreover, that there would be more insults like the recent one as long as he could pass my gate. I determined therefore to go away, as I had planned earlier, to that temple in the western moun-tains and to do so before he emerged from his penance. On the Fourth, the day I believed the penance was to end, I hastily put together what I would need for the trip. Under one of the quilts someone found an envelope containing some medicine which I had been in the habit of taking in the morning and which I had put away before I left for my fa-ther's. Everyone gathered around to see what it might be, and I wrote on the envelope, "'Thus disappears even the refuge under the quilt; and where is one to go now?'"[131]

I also wrote a letter to the Prince: "I suppose you will say that I am doing it to make you call.[132] I have decided in any case to leave today for a temple where you will not be able to parade back and forth in front of my gate. Even this you will consider an uninvited outburst, I know."

I sent it over with the boy, who indicated that he would like to ask after his father before we shut ourselves off, and I instructed him to say, if anyone questioned him, that I had left in some haste and that he was to follow after me.

"What you say is of course just," the Prince answered, no doubt thinking me rash and rather badly organized. "But

tell me where you intend to go. And it is not a good time of
the year for such trips. Take my advice at least this once and
give it up. I shall be right over. I want to talk to you. Most
unkind of you—'You overturn the bed just when I had
thought to rest comfortably.' ''

At the suggestion that he was on his way over, I set out
with even more haste.

The mountain road was not particularly striking. For me
it was crowded with associations, however, and I could not
help weeping. We had traveled it together a number of
times, and there had been that time, just at this season, when
he had played truant from court and we had spent several
days together in this same temple.[133] I had only three attendants with me now.

We stopped first at the priests' quarters. In the garden,
bounded by a low wattle fence, were a great many plants
whose names I did not know and a few forlorn peonies, their
blossoms already fallen. The season of fading flowers will
come, I thought, and nothing is to stop it.[134]

Just as I had finished purifying myself and was about to
start for the main hall, a messenger ran up with a letter from
a woman of my household: ''A letter has come from the
Prince. 'His Highness,' the messenger said, 'is getting ready
to come over.[135] Please keep Her Ladyship from leaving before he arrives.' I told him how you had hurried off and said
that a number of attendants had followed. 'But he has been
so worried about her,' the man answered. 'How can I tell
him of this?' I then described your recent retreat and your
loneliness all these months. 'Well, I must let him know immediately what has happened,' he said and hurried off weeping. You will of course hear from the Prince, or perhaps see
him, and it might be well to be prepared.''[136]

I was annoyed at the dramatics and at the woman's flighti-
ness.[137] All this excitement even though the usual defilement[138] would in any case force me to leave the temple in a
couple of days.

I washed myself and hurried up to the main hall. It being
warm, I left the door open and looked out. The hall was
situated on an eminence in a sort of mountain basin. It was

heavily wooded and the view was most effective, although it was already growing dark and there was no moon. The priests made preparations for the early watch,[139] and I began my prayers, still with the door open.

Just as the conch shells announced the end of the services, there was a clamor at the main gate. I knew the Prince had arrived. I quickly lowered the blinds and, looking out, saw two or three torches among the trees.

"I have come to take your mother back," he said to the boy, who went down to meet him. "I have suffered a defilement, though, and cannot get out. Where shall I have them go to pick her up?"

The boy told me what he had said, and I was quite at a loss to know how to handle such madness. "What can you be thinking of," I sent back, "to come off on such a weird expedition? Really, I intend to stay here only the night. And it would not be wise for you to defile the temple. Please go back immediately—it must be getting late."

Those were the first of a great number of messages the boy had to deliver that night, up and down a flight of stairs that must have been more than a hundred yards long.[140] My attendants, sentimental things, said they found him most pathetic.

Finally he came up in tears: "He says it is all my fault—that I am a poor one not to make a better case for him. He is really in a rage." But I was firm. I could not possibly go down yet, I said.

"All right, all right," the Prince stormed. "In my condition I can't stay all night. There is no help for it—hitch the oxen."

I was greatly relieved. But the boy said that he would like to go back to the city with his father, and that he would probably not come again. He went off weeping. I was quite desolate. How could he, whom I had come most to rely on, say such a thing? But I held my peace. Then, after everyone had left, he came back alone.

He was choked with tears. "He says I am to stay until I am sent for."

I felt extremely sorry for the boy, but I tried to distract

him by ridiculing his weakness. Surely he did not think his father would abandon him too, I said.

It was two in the morning, and the road back to the city was a long one. As the dawn came on, my people remarked on how sad it was to see the Prince off here in the mountains, so much more poorly appointed than when he moved about in the city. Probably in his haste he had not been able to get together a decent escort.

In the morning I sent a messenger off to the city on some business. The boy, worried about the incident of the previous evening, went along to ask after his father, and I sent a letter with him: "I kept thinking all night of your somewhat grotesque visit, and of how late it must have been when you got back to the city. I could only pray to the Buddha to see you home safely. When I consider the intentions that prompted you to come all this way, I feel that I could not abuse your kindness, and it has become difficult for me to return." On the margin I added: "I thought a great deal on the way here of how we once traveled the same road together. I shall go back down to the city as soon as possible." I sent it off attached to a moss-covered pine branch. A thick mist, a cloud almost, was rising in the early-morning sky as I wrote.

Toward noon the boy came back. The Prince had been out, he said, and he had left the letter with a servant. There would probably have been no answer anyway, I thought.

Thus I spent the days in the usual observances and the nights praying before the main Buddha. Since the place was surrounded by hills, and there seemed no danger of my being seen, I kept the blinds up; but once, so great still was my lack of self-possession, I hastily started to lower them when an unseasonal thrush burst into song in a dead tree nearby.[141]

Then the expected defilement approached, and I saw I should have to leave. But in the city a rumor had spread that I had become a nun, and I knew I could not be comfortable there. I decided therefore to withdraw to a house some distance below the temple. My aunt came to visit me there, but she found it a strange and unsettling place.

Five or six days after my removal came the night of full moon. The scene was a lovely one. The moon flooded through the trees, while over in the shadow of the mountain great swarms of fireflies wheeled about. An uninhibited cuckoo made me think ironically of how once, long ago when I had had no worries, I had waited with some annoyance for a cuckoo that refused to repeat his call.[142] And then suddenly, so near at hand that it seemed almost to be knocking on the door, came the drumming of a moor hen.[143] All in all it was a spot that stirred in one the deepest of emotions.

There was no word from the Prince. But I had come here by my own choice, and I was content. I could not help brooding nonetheless over the load of karma that had driven me to such a hermitage. Also I was distressed that the boy seemed so apathetic. There had been no alternative to bringing him with me, since I knew of no one with whom I could leave him. All day long he stayed shut up in the house, and as I watched him try unsuccessfully to get down the rough food to which I had condemned us—it was all right for me, this eating of pine needles, but what of him?—I would feel the tears welling up. It was annoying that, even when I had achieved a certain peace of mind, I should still be so prone to weep.

In the evening came the booming of the great sunset bells, and the hum of the cicadas, and the choruses of small bells from the temples in the hills around us, chiming in one after another as though afraid to be left out, and the chanting of sutras from the shrine on the hill in front of us.[144] It all filled me with the deepest, most poignant thoughts.

Time was rather heavy on my hands. Once I went out on the veranda, but the boy beckoned me in as though he hoped to keep my melancholy from getting the best of me. "What is the matter?" I asked. He avoided a direct answer and only stammered, "It is no good—I am very sleepy."

"I have felt rather strongly," I said, coming in, "that I should like to die, but the thought of you has kept me alive until now. And where am I to go from here? Shall I do as the gossips say I have done and become a nun? That would be better than quite vanishing from the world, and perhaps you will think kindly of me and come to see me often enough to keep me from getting lonely. I do not think I was wrong in coming here, but when I see how thin this wretched food has made you I am most unhappy. It would be nice to know that if I did become a nun I would still have your father to fall back on, but he is most unreliable. Ah, I have so much to worry about!''

The boy was sobbing and did not answer.

Five days or so later the defilement passed, and I returned to the temple.

Presently my aunt had to go back to the city. So lonely that I was almost frightened, I watched her carriage pull away and disappear among the trees, and then suddenly I was taken with a dizziness and a sharp throbbing in the temples. I called in the priests for spells and incantations, and as I listened to their chants in the growing dusk, I fell again to brooding over my wretchedness. Long ago, when I had seen people such as I was now, I had thought them most depressing and had painted exaggerated[145] pictures of them and, unable to restrain myself, had spoken out freely on how very unpleasant I found them. I never dreamed that I might someday become one of them myself, and yet here I was, not a whit different. Perhaps it had all been a premonition, a warning.

As I lay there, my sister and my aunt came in[146] and knelt beside me. ''We tried to imagine, back in the city, what things must be like here,'' my sister said, already in tears, ''but I see it is worse than we thought. We have hardly been able to sleep for worrying over you.''[147]

My situation here was my own doing, and I tried to control myself; but soon I too was weeping. Alternately laughing and weeping, we talked until morning.

Since my aunt[148] was in a great hurry, the two of them returned to the city the next day, but my sister promised to come again. ''Do you intend to stay forever?'' she asked sadly. They looked most forlorn as they left the temple.

Feeling somewhat better, I went out to see them off. Just as they pulled away there came a great clamor indicating the approach of someone important. It has started again, I thought. A procession came up, very elegant and reminiscent of the city. There were two fine carriages, some exceedingly handsome and variously dressed men, and a number of horses which they proceeded to tie up here and there around the court. The party was loaded down with food and supplies and passed out handsome presents of cloth and robes to the rather shabby priests who kept the services at the place.

"It has largely been the Prince's idea for us to come," the leader of the group[149] said. "'I went myself, but it did no good,' he said to us, 'and very likely I would have no better success if I were to go again. And so I have to reconsider. You fellows go seek an audience[150] with her and see what you can do. And while you are at it you might find out what those priests are up to with all that sutra business.' That is what he said, and really who could stand this for a lifetime? If the gossips were right and you had become a nun, well, things would be very sad, I suppose. But you will look pretty foolish going back by yourself after you have held out against all his urging. He will come again, and if you don't go back with him then people will really laugh."

His pompous chatter went on and on.

The people at my house[151] too had sent along great stores of provisions. It was kind of them to do so, but to receive such attentions off here in the mountains served only to emphasize the point to which I had fallen.

"We are in a hurry to get back," the same talkative person said toward evening. "Certainly we won't force you to go with us, but it hardly seems a good idea for you to go on with nothing definite in mind. When do you think you might be ready to leave?"

"Really, at the moment I have no plans at all, and when I have something to do in the city I shall go back," I answered. "I am here only because I have been bored and have had nothing else to do."

Even if I did go back, I thought, it would be as if I were a nun. Perhaps someone who thought I might be persuaded to stay here had prompted him to adopt that challenging tone. Yet what in fact could I do back in the city?[152]

"Well, I will stay here for the time being in any case."

"It may be all right for you to stay off here with no ideas of going back," he remarked as a final thrust. "But think of the boy. You have dragged him off against his will, and he is the saddest victim of the whole affair." He climbed weeping into his carriage.

My people went out to see them off, and he warned them that they too were falling from the Prince's favor and that they would be held responsible if they did not get me back to the city immediately. The departure of this elegant party made our temple seem lonelier than ever. My people all looked as though they were about to burst into tears.

Thus from every direction I was prodded and harassed, but I remained firm. My father, the one man whose opinion, whatever it might be, I could not ignore, was still away in the provinces. I had written to him of the pilgrimage, and I was much relieved when he answered that he saw nothing wrong with my slipping away and praying quietly for a while.

I began to wonder whether the Prince himself might not have had an ulterior motive in sending that envoy. Certainly his pleas did not seem worth taking at their face value, and maybe he did not want me to come back at all. He had gone home in that great rage, and even though he knew how I was living, he had sent not even a note since. If the very worst were to happen to me, I could not know what to expect from him. And if I were to go from here to some retreat even deeper in the mountains, he would probably not come to take me back.

On the Fifteenth, a fast day,[153] I persuaded the boy to go back to the city for some decent food. Later in the day, as I sat gazing out at the sky and thinking many thoughts, a black thunderstorm came up and a high wind began to roar through the pines. He would just be starting back, I thought in dismay. But presently, perhaps because of my prayers, the storm passed over and he arrived uninjured. He had left the city at the first sound of thunder, he said, fearing that the rain might be a bad one. The thought of him starting out alone in the storm with no one to restrain or advise him touched me deeply.

He brought a letter from the Prince: "Ever since my return from that unfortunate trip, I have felt that if I were to repeat it the results would only be the same. Perhaps you really have grown tired of the world and decided to cut yourself off from it, but if you should decide to come back, let me know and I shall come for you. In the meantime, since you seem to dread my visits so, I shall keep my distance." There was a letter too from someone else, which said in part: "Do you intend to stay on there indefinitely? As the days go by, I think about you more and more."

I answered the next day: "I do not really intend to stay here 'indefinitely,' but somehow as I have sat here thinking the days have gone by. 'Who could have foreseen that I should be here joining my laments with the voices of the vesper bells?'"

A second note came the following day: "I find it impossible to put down my feelings. It was as though I were being torn apart, to read your verse about the vesper bells. 'And what of us, still left in the gloomy world? It is sadder to read such poems than to write them.'"

I was much moved. Then one of the several people I had left to tend the house sent this letter to a woman who had come with me (I do not know what precisely the point was): "I have always thought Her Ladyship rather remarkable, but my admiration for her has grown since you have all gone away. I can imagine, therefore, the affection and sorrow you yourself must feel. We 'low-born ones,'[154] though we may not be good at expressing ourselves, can understand a tragedy such as hers. 'When even one who has renounced the world and is not concerned with its sorrows thinks of retiring to the mountains, how much worse must it be with her!'"

The lady to whom it was addressed brought it in and read it to me, and again I was much moved. So it is that at such times the most insignificant things will affect one deeply. I told her to answer it immediately, and she sent off this: "I should have thought that 'among the low-born'[155] few would be able to understand such a situation, but when I read your letter to Her Ladyship she could not keep back her tears, and I should like you to imagine how I felt as I watched her. 'Sad are the memories, and the dew under the groves of these deep mountains lies heavy.'"

My son was most anxious that I should answer the Prince's letter. He was afraid of his father's displeasure and offered to deliver my answer himself. "And what made you think I wouldn't?" I said, and wrote: "I intended to answer your letter immediately, but it seemed cruel to send the boy to the city again. I really can't tell you when I shall be leaving here. I haven't made up my own mind. I find it tiresome, trying to imagine why you should suggest that I am frightening you off; and I shall say no more."

The boy started out, and again the rain and thunder came up. I waited with great apprehension, but toward evening, when it had quieted down a bit, he came back safely. The storm had been particularly bad in the vicinity of Misama,[156] he said.

"Your letter indicates that you may be losing control of yourself," the Prince wrote among other things. "I wonder if it might not be the result of that constant praying."

The following day a distant relative came to see me, bringing numerous boxes of food. "What could have prompted you to do this?" she asked. "Really, unless there is some extraordinarily good reason for it, it does not seem to me at all proper."

I proceeded to tell her in the greatest detail the circumstances that had forced me to leave the city, and presently she was reduced to tears and agreed that I was quite justified.

We talked all day, and in the evening, after the usual dreary good-byes and just as the vesper bells were ringing, she started for the city. She is a perceptive person, capable of real feeling, and I think my problem must have been heavy on her mind all the way back.

I felt a new pang of loneliness the next day when she sent a store of provisions as though for someone going on a long

trip. With them was a letter describing the gloom of her return trip: "I was beside myself on the way back, thinking of
what you said. I had known of course that you were off in the
gloomy forests, but now to see you! 'Were yours the marriage the world usually knows, would we then find ourselves cutting through the rank summer grasses?' When I
knew I should have to leave you and start back, my eyes were
quite blinded with tears. Indeed you have cause to grieve.
'Who was it made you travel the mountain road to Narutaki?'"

It was written in the greatest detail, as though we were
talking together. (Narutaki is the name of the river in front
of the temple there.)[157]

For my answer, I wrote down everything as it came to
mind: "I wonder what can have brought you to visit me in
a place like this. 'Those deep summer grasses do not stand
comparison with my deep sorrows.' I have not decided when
I shall go back to the city, but letters such as yours fill me
with disturbing thoughts. 'You ask about me. Well, at
Narutaki there are clear waters that return not whence they
came.'[158] So you see I have a precedent if I do decide to stay."

Then I had a letter from the Lady Jōganden,[159] to which I
sent a long, rather gloomy reply. On the envelope I wrote
"From the Western Mountains," and I wondered what she
would think of it. On her next letter she wrote "From
Toba."[160] It was as though the exotic place names gave us
something in common.

Some days later a poem was delivered unobtrusively[161]
from a man who seemed to be making the pilgrimage
through the peaks of Yamato to Kumano:[162] "So it is even in
the foothills; and perhaps, friend or stranger, one can imagine the deep loneliness of the cloud-covered mountains."[163]

One day at about noon there was a neighing of horses at
the main gate, and a stir as though a sizable party had arrived. Several men of not very high rank approached through
the trees, and I was told that they were in attendance on the
Captain of the Guards.[164] Calling for my son, the Captain
sent in his apologies for not having paid his respects earlier.
He was a handsome figure indeed as he stood taking his ease

in the shade and I suspected that he was making a particular effort to impress my sister (she was with me again).

"I am very happy that you are here," I sent back. "Please come up immediately. I shall pray to the Buddha for your happiness and success."

He leaned on the railing to rinse his hands[165] and presently came in.

We talked of a great many things, and I asked if he remembered having seen me once years before.[166] "Of course," he replied. "How should I have forgotten it— even though I have been so neglectful since." And as I thought of the days when I had known him as a child, I found myself unable to say anything lest my voice break. Apparently conscious of the tension, he too was silent for a time.

Then, though he evidently misjudged the source of my emotion, he undertook to comfort me: "It is quite understandable that you should feel this way. But you needn't be afraid. There is no danger that he will abandon you." And after a pause he added: "He has instructed me to see whether I can make you reconsider what you are doing."

"But why should he have asked you to do that? I intend to go back soon in any case," I answered.

"If that is so, why not go back today? I can escort you immediately. And it has been especially sad to see my brother[167] have to hurry back up here on the few days he has been in the city."

But I showed no disposition to listen to his arguments, and he started for the city after resting awhile. I thought that now surely everyone who could be expected to visit me had come.

Then, after a time, I received several letters from the city. They all said the same thing. It appeared that the Prince was starting out to see me again, and that if I did not go back with him this time public opinion would label my behavior completely outrageous; that this was surely the last time he would come after me; and that if, after he had thus done everything possible to move me, I should come weakly back to the city myself, I would be publicly laughed at.

My father had just that day come back from the provinces, and he hurried up to see me. ''I had thought it would not be unwise for you to go away for a little while by yourself,'' he said, ''but now that I see how the boy has wasted away I think it would be best to return. I can take you back either today or tomorrow, whichever you prefer. I shall come for you whenever you say.''

It was clear that he was ordering me home. I felt quite drained of strength.

''Well, tomorrow then,'' he said and started for the city.

My mind jumped about like the fisherman's bob in the poem[168]—what could I do? And then came the usual shouting, and I knew that the Prince had arrived. This time there was no hesitation. He marched straight in. I pulled up a screen to hide behind, but it was no use.

''Terrible,'' he exclaimed, as he watched me burning incense and fingering my beads, the sutras spread before me. ''Worse even than I had expected. You really do seem to have run to an extreme. I thought you might be ready to leave by this time, but now I suspect that it would be a sin and a crime to take you back.'' And, turning to my son, ''How about it? Do you feel like staying on?''

''I don't like the idea at all,'' the boy answered, his eyes on the floor, ''but what can we do?''

''Well, I leave it to you. If you think she should go back, have the carriage brought up.''

And almost before he had finished speaking, the boy began dashing about, picking things up, poking them into bags, loading the carts, tearing the curtains down and rolling them into bundles. I was taken quite by surprise and could only watch helplessly. The Prince was most pleased with himself. Now and then he would exchange an amused wink with the boy.

''Well, we have everything cleaned up,'' he finally said. ''There is not much for you to do but come with us. Tell your Buddha politely that you are leaving. That is the thing to do, I hear.'' He seemed to think it all a great joke.

I was too numb to answer, but somehow I managed to keep the tears back. The carriage was brought up, and still I held out. The Prince had come at about four. At dark, when I still showed no sign of moving, he turned to the boy.

"All right, all right, I am going back," he exclaimed. "I leave everything to you."

The boy, almost in tears, took my hand and pleaded with me to get in, and finally, since nothing else seemed possible, I allowed myself to be taken away, quite in a daze. Outside the main gate we divided up for the trip back, and the Prince got in with me. His repartee was most witty, but I was unable to answer. My sister was riding with us, however—she felt that it would be all right, since it was already dark—and now and then she took up the conversation.

We reached the city at about ten in the evening. My people had of course known of his trip and my probable return and had cleaned the place thoroughly and left the gates open for us. Barely conscious, I lay down behind a curtain. Immediately one of my women came bustling up. "I thought of gathering seeds from the pinks," she said, "but the plants died. And then one of your bamboos fell over, but I had it put back up again." I thought it would be better to discuss these problems some other time and did not answer.

The Prince, whom I had thought to be asleep, took everything in and burst out in a voice loud enough to be heard by my sister in the next room, "Listen to that, will you! She goes off to find salvation, and when she comes back they tell her the pinks are in the pink,[169] and the bamboo is doing well too! What could be more to the point!" Everyone laughed loudly. I too thought the report on the garden not entirely appropriate, but I gave no sign that I was amused.

Later in the evening, he started up. "What direction is forbidden today?" he asked, and when they consulted the horoscope there appeared not a doubt that my direction was the unlucky one. "What a nuisance! I shall have to go away somewhere, I suppose. Why don't we go together? Somewhere near-by will do."

But I thought the idea quite insane, whatever punishment he might expect for the transgression, and gave no sign of being prepared to move. "Well, in any case I shall have to be off," he said. He seemed really annoyed at having to go.

"I shall come sometime when the direction is luckier, only now I seem to have a penance to look forward to."[170]

Early the next morning I received a letter: "It was most unpleasant to have to leave last night. I meant to tell you that I think it would be wise for you to stop your fasting immediately.[171] Really, the boy should look after you better."

It no longer made much difference to me what he said; and yet I waited with strange impatience for the day his penance was to end.[172] Six days went by, and there was no word from him. On the Third of the Seventh Month some servants came from his house. "It seems that the Prince is to come today. He told us we should be here," they reported, and my people went noisily to work at all sorts of jobs about the house that had been left undone for days. A ridiculous burst of activity, I thought. In the evening his servants too began to have doubts. His carriage was ready, and why had he not come, they wondered. Finally one of my people went over to see what was happening and came back with the report that the carriage had been unhitched and dismantled and the escort broken up.

I hardly knew what to say. It was a repetition of the incidents that had so hurt me before. If I had been allowed to stay on in the mountains, I thought, I would not have been subjected again to such treatment. My people loudly denounced the Prince for this new insult.

Well, he was like the man who visits his "bride" for three nights and disappears. I would feel a little better, I thought, if he would only tell me why.

I had a caller, rather an untimely one, but as I talked with her my mind was diverted somewhat from my worries. The boy went to ask after the Prince the next day and was told that he had not felt well the evening before, that he had suddenly been seized with severe pains and had been unable to go out. I would be happier without such excuses, I thought. I was suffering from the usual defilement in any case, and would have been satisfied if he had simply given an indication that he wanted to call.

A very touching letter came from the Lady Jōganden,[173] who seemed to think that I was still in the country: "What whim can have led you to put yourself away in that sad place? I have been told that, in spite of your being so far off, he still comes to see you, and I am therefore somewhat puzzled by your statement that you have parted. 'If the Imose River still follows its old course, we should still see the usual visits.' ''[174]

"I had hoped to stay in the mountains until autumn," I answered, "but I have reached a point where I can be happy neither in the mountains nor in the city, and now I am back here leading the same meaningless life again. I should have thought that my sorrows in 'that sad place' were like 'mountain grasses no one knows of,'[175] and I wonder what you may have heard. On the matter you refer to in your poem—'I may indeed grieve as one abandoned; the waters that flow between Imo and Se, you must remember, are not as constant as they might be.' ''[176]

On the Fifth he was in penance, and on the Sixth my direction was forbidden; but the day after I found myself, quite incorrigibly, waiting for the evening.[177] Late in the night he appeared. He had all manner of excuses for his recent behavior. He had intended to come earlier in the evening, he said, but he had had to send the people at the other house away to avoid some transgression or other,[178] and, that done, he had come flying to me without another thought for them. His manner was guileless as ever, and I was unspeakably irritated. Early the next morning he went off to see about the people he had sent away the night before.

Another week passed. My father was planning a pilgrimage to Hase and suggested that I go with him, and together we went off to purify ourselves. We were not left alone, however. At about noon a procession came up noisily. "Someone has opened the far gate," the owner of the place[179] said in astonishment, and soon the Prince rushed in. He stayed at his leisure and returned the following day, making himself generally objectionable, knocking over incense, throwing rosaries up on high shelves, and otherwise behaving in a most remarkable manner.

Seven or eight days later, at about ten in the morning, we started for Hase. We reached the late Inspector's[180] Uji mansion at about two in the afternoon. Our retinue was large and gay, but I could not repress a certain loneliness as I looked around at the house and grounds. This was the estate into which he had put so much thought and effort, and now, exactly a year after his death, it was going to ruin.

The caretaker invited us in for lunch. The furnishings seemed still to be those left by the Inspector: drapes and blinds, woven-bark screens,[181] and saffron curtains[182] on black-persimmon frames. It was all in the best of taste, and all very sad.

A strong wind came up. My head throbbed from the strain of the trip, but I had a wind-screen put up and went to look at the river. As it grew dark the cormorant boats, each with its flare, began rowing up and down over the whole surface of the river, and presently I forgot my headache. I raised the blind, and, as I gazed out, I thought of how, on the trip to Hase I had made by myself, the Inspector had been alive, and the Prince had exchanged letters with him and no doubt had a good conversation. And now he was dead. Where is it ordained that things must be so ephemeral?

"'What is it that tosses about, burning in the night?'" I murmured to myself. "'The cormorant boats, and then my restless heart.'" Unable to sleep, I watched until past midnight. When I looked again it was dawn, and the cormorant boats had given way to the boats that work the traps.

We started out again early in the morning. Nieno Pond and the Izumi River and the other places along the way were just as I had remembered them and served to emphasize how uncertain my own fortunes were by contrast. The noisiness of our procession made meditation difficult, but the way seemed deeply meaningful. We had lunch at the grove of Yōtate; everyone seemed to eat with good appetite.[183]

In order to do homage at the Kasuga Shrine we stopped that night at a wretched temple, and the next morning started out in a driving rain. It did us no good to be under the Mountain of the Umbrellas[184]—most of the party got thoroughly drenched. But we made it to the shrine, gave offerings, and started again in the direction of Hase. We had the carriages pulled up to the paling of the Asuka Temple and looked in while a votive light was being offered. The trees were thick, the garden well kept, and the water cool and inviting. Indeed, as the old song suggests, one could do worse than to stop at the Well of Asuka.[185]

The rain only got worse as it drew on toward evening. At Tsubaichi we made the usual preparations for the ascent to the temple, starting out again as darkness came on. The wind soon blew our torches out, and we pushed on through the black night. It was like a murky trip in a nightmare. I even began to wonder whether we would survive. But somehow we reached the purification hall and went inside. The rain was no longer audible, only a great rush of water, the river, I was told.

I was in acute discomfort as we climbed to the main hall. There were many things I ought to be thinking about, but I was much too depressed to collect them into anything coherent. The dawn came without my having made any of my supplications to the Buddha. And still the rain went on.

We felt that we had endured enough for one pilgrimage and determined to start back in the daylight. As we passed the grove where one is forbidden to talk, my people, as such people will, gestured and mouthed elaborately at one another to be quiet. They looked for all the world like gulping fish. It was irresistibly funny.

One usually changes from pilgrim's fare at Tsubaichi, but I felt that I should like to keep the fast for a while yet. From Tsubaichi on, however, there were invitations which we could not refuse and which delayed our passage. As we handed out courtesy gifts[186] the local gentry seemed to exhaust their ingenuity in entertaining us.

The waters of the Izumi River had risen, and we debated how to proceed. The men were for plunging ahead in the usual fashion. It was true we had acquired a skillful boatman from Uji, but boats were such a nuisance, they said. The women, however, were in favor of a boat trip and won the argument. We floated happily down the river with the oarsmen leading the songs. Near Uji we changed again to carriages,[187] and at Uji we stopped for the night, since the capital lay in an unlucky direction.

I wanted to watch the cormorant boats at close range—
the river was alive with them—and, ordering a stand set up,
took cushions and went down to the river bank.[188] The
boats were practically at my feet. For the first time I could
see the birds actually taking fish—it was wonderfully interesting. I was exhausted from the journey, but I was uncon-
scious of the passage of time until my attendants began
prodding me to go back to the house. There was nothing
more to be seen, they said. I went with them, but the fishing
continued through the night, and I was far from tired of
watching. Now and then I would doze off, only to start up at
a rapping on the prow of a boat, which seemed almost as
though designed purposely to wake me. We saw in the
morning that there had been a large catch of trout, and we
decided that it would make excellent gifts back in the
city.

It was well on in the day when we started out again, and
we reached my father's house after dark. I wanted to move
on immediately, but as my people were tired we stayed there
overnight.

At noon the next day there was a letter from the Prince:
"I thought of going to meet you, but then it wasn't as if you
had gone out alone this time, and I thought too that my
presence would only complicate matters. Are you back at
your house yet? I shall be over immediately."

I hurried home, urged on by my people, and shortly he
appeared. Perhaps even he was moved by memories of our
younger years. But he left early the next morning, ostensibly
to look after the preparations for the wrestling banquet.[189]
Though the excuse was credible enough, it was sad to think
that he still found such excuses necessary.

He seems to have had four days or so of penance thereafter. I saw him a couple of times, and presently the Eighth
Month came. The wrestling meet out of the way, I heard
that he had gone off to a mountain temple for some services.
I had nothing from him for three or four days, and then, one
rainy day, this letter came: "I have been told that when one
goes off to the mountains people sometimes write to him.
There are those who say that it is sad when people do not."

"No one knows better than I the truth of what you say," I replied. "I thought perhaps sooner than anyone of inquiring after you, but then I decided that it might be well for you to know what loneliness is. As for me: when one has wept oneself dry, one tends to be indifferent to distant clouds."[190] A reply came immediately.

About three days later, well along in the evening, I saw him. He had come back that day, he said. We had reached a point where I was no longer able to tell, even under the best of circumstances, what he was thinking, and I lapsed into a stiff unresponsiveness. He of course continued to pretend that he had done nothing wrong. I saw him occasionally, once a week or so.

The scenery those days was most moving. A strong wind blew for some days toward the end of the Ninth Month, and between showers the high mountains gleamed a clear, bright blue, as though perhaps hail had fallen on them. "Wouldn't it be nice," I suggested, "to go on a pilgrimage somewhere and take in the autumn scenery?"

"A splendid idea," my women exclaimed. "Let's go off again to Hase, quietly this time."

"But let us see first what results we have had from that wretched trip to Ishiyama.[191] Then possibly next spring we can go to Hase. I should, I suppose, still be stretching out my dreary life." And I added a poem:

There was a time when I complained
That my sleeves were wet with tears,
But now I am drenched with the autumn rain,
And the flooding on of the years.

This was for me a melancholy period. Life seemed pointless, the monotony was unbroken: a listless rising and going to bed, no variation for twenty days on end. What had brought me to this, I wondered. But there was after all nothing to be done about it.

One morning the roof was covered with frost, and all the children in the place, still in their night clothes, scampered about blessing themselves against frostbite. "Ah, it is cold," they cried, their sleeves against their mouths. "A frost like this even beats a snow." It was strange to think that these children were dependent on me, weak and helpless though I was.

Thus a strangely saddening month went by, and the Eleventh Month began with the same uninterrupted monotony. On the Twentieth I saw him, but for more than twenty days afterwards there were only one or two letters. Although I could hardly have been called content, I had reached a certain resignation, and I no longer had the strength of spirit to worry about his coolness.[192]

On the Sixteenth of the Twelfth Month another letter came, a remarkably friendly one. "I have had eight days of penance, but I should like to call today," it said among other things. Suddenly the sky clouded over, and as I looked out I wondered whether he really would consider coming on a day like this. It was still raining fiercely in the evening. I felt more and more that I could not expect him. And I thought of the days when a rain such as this would never have troubled him, and, weeping and unable to restrain myself, I sent a messenger with this verse: "We are told that no rain can stop Lord Isonokami;[193] and is it different with you?"

At about the time I felt my messenger should have arrived, I sensed the approach of someone at the south side of the house, where the shutters had been lowered. No one else could have heard it. I myself had only the vaguest feeling that something was astir. And presently the Prince came hurrying in through the side door.[194] The rain was falling so heavily that at first I could hear nothing, and then there was a shouting as his carriage was pulled in.

He announced that, although he had perhaps given me cause for dissatisfaction, I must forgive him because of his having fought his way through the storm this evening. His manner was most persuasive. The following day, he said, a certain direction in which he often went[195] was forbidden him, and the day after that he went into penance again— there was no avoiding it. The message I had sent had, to my relief, apparently not reached him.

The rain stopped during the night, and he left with a promise to return in the evening. With that other direction forbidden him, I rather thought he might. But I was disappointed. The next day came an apology: "I had a caller last night until so late that I canceled my visit to you and had sutras read instead. You were as annoyed as you usually are, I suppose."

"I wondered where you might have gone, with that taboo hanging over you," I answered. My letter was rather a long one, and I ended it with a verse: "Can it be because she has lost the help of the god of the plantain leaves that the rain frog is thus abandoned?"[196] He had given me the sobriquet "rain frog"[197] on my return from the western mountains.

I heard that he was going to that woman's[198] every night. Even now I could not accept the idea with equanimity. New Year's Eve came, and so another year had passed—how swiftly they all passed. I did not join in the devil-chasing,[199] but everyone else, young and old alike, lustily shouted away the devils, quite determined, it seemed, to make this a house without sorrow. A heavy snow was falling, and I hoped only that everything would melt away with it.

*

* Book Three

*

THUS began the Third Year of Tenroku.[1] Whatever trying things might come later, I thought, I would at least begin the year with a calm mind. I saw my son off to the palace, and as he descended into the garden and bowed,[2] I felt a surge of pride and affection that moved me almost to tears. I wanted to have New Year services of some kind, but unfortunately from that evening I was expecting the usual defilement. What ill things might it be a harbinger of, this defilement at the outset of the year? But however hateful people might be, I told myself, I would not let them bother me, and with that thought I felt a certain peace.

The coming-of-age ceremony for the Emperor was held on the Third, and there was much talk of white horses[3] and such, but I was not feeling well and took little interest. On about the Eighth I saw the Prince. He left early because, he said, there were those incessant ceremonies and festivals to tend to.

While his men were waiting for him, one of them sent this verse in to my women: "The lid of this Shimozuke pail is most unsatisfying; it is empty and cannot reflect your image."[4] They sent the lid back full of saké and fruit, and with it a poem: "This lid has no body, and the sincerity of your song I suspect is similarly defective."

Because of my ill-defined position, I was less occupied than most with the rituals that covered the first half of the month.

On the Fourteenth the Prince sent an outer robe for me to do over. Since he specified when it was to be finished, I thought I might proceed at my leisure. A messenger came the next morning to hurry me, however, and a verse formed in my mind: "Must you rush me so? I had thought that I might have this robe in place of you."

I nonetheless finished it, and returned it with no comment. "You have done it after all, and very nicely," he said, "but what a shame you did not wear it to think of me."

That seemed a bit smug, and I felt it called for a retort: "'Hurry, hurry, you may say; but with old things like me and this Chinese robe it is no use.'"

Thereafter, with the excitement of the New Year lists,[5] I heard nothing more from him.

On the Twenty-third, before the shutters were raised, one of my women pushed open the end door and announced that snow had fallen during the night, and just then we heard the first song of the thrush. I felt too old and worn out, however, to recite the usual, trite verses.

The New Year lists were published on the Twenty-fifth, and the Prince, I heard, was made a Senior Councilor.[6] I knew that his promotion would keep him from me more than ever, and when people came around to congratulate me it was almost as if they were joking. My son, however, appeared more delighted than he could say.

The following day the Prince sent a note: "Does this happy event mean nothing to you? Is that why you have sent no congratulations?" And toward the end of the month: "Has something happened to you? We have been very busy here, but it is not kind of you to ignore me." Thus my silence had the effect of making him the petitioner, a position which until then had been exclusively mine. It did not seem to occur to him that he might be at fault.

"It is sad that your duties keep you so busy," I answered. I was sure he had no intention of visiting me.

The days went by, and it became clear that I was right. But I had finally learned not to let his silence bother me. I slept very well at night.

Then one evening after I had gone to bed I was startled by a most unusual pounding outside. Someone opened the gate. I waited rather nervously, and presently the Prince was at the end door demanding to be let in. My people, all in night dress, scurried about for shelter. I was no better dressed than they, but I crawled to the door and let him in.

"You so seldom come any more even to pass the time of day," I said, "that the door seems to have grown little stiff."

"It is because you are always locking me out that I do not come," he retorted pleasantly. And how would one answer that?

Toward dawn a fierce wind began to roar through the pines. Some considerate god or Buddha, I thought, must have taken care that this was not one of the many nights I had to spend alone. The next morning, the First of the Second Month, a quiet rain was falling. Even after we raised the shutters he showed none of the usual impatience to be off. Perhaps it was the rain that made him so docile. I knew he would not stay all day, however, and presently he asked whether his escort had come yet. He was dressed informally in a soft under-robe[7] and a starched cloak,[8] tied loosely with a sash. My people were about to offer him breakfast, but he refused good-naturedly: "I have not been in the habit of having breakfast here, and why should I begin now?" The boy brought in his sword and presented it kneeling, and he went out quietly for a look about the garden. "See what a rough job they've made of burning the dead grass," he said.

Shortly his carriage came up equipped with rain awnings.[9] His men held it lightly in place for him, and he climbed in, pulled the curtains, and proceeded through the inner gate.[10] As I heard his outrunners clearing the way in the distance I felt a pang of envy at the ladies who were more frequently honored than I with all this magnificence.

We had not raised the shutters for several days because of the wind. As I looked out at the rain, I noticed that here and there in the battered garden patches of green were beginning to show through. Toward noon the wind came up again, this time from the opposite direction, and the sky began to clear. Strangely depressed, I continued to gaze out until dark.

On the Third snow began to fall. It continued even after

it had piled four and five inches deep.[11] I looked out with the blinds raised, and I heard murmurs of "How cold it is!" A strong wind blew up. A melancholy world it seemed.

On the Eighth, after the weather had cleared, I went for a visit to my father's house. The place was full of young people who laughed and sang and played in well-chosen modes on the *koto*[12] and *biwa*[13] the whole night through. I felt calm and relaxed when they left the next morning.

A letter came from the Prince: "I have had a long penance and have been very busy at court. I should like to call today, immediately, however."

He would come immediately—so he said, but, forgotten and shut off from the world, I did not think he would really bother to visit me. Still I sent an answer, and toward noon, when the house[14] and all of us were in complete disorder, a stir at the gate announced his arrival. I received him in the most extreme consternation, quite unable to collect myself. He ate a little and then left; the Kasuga Festival[15] was to take place the following day and the day after that, and he would be kept busy sending off the court emissary, he explained. His dress was just as it should be, and his escort large, and off they went, grandly shouting away everyone on the road.

My people quickly clustered around: "What can he have thought of us, undressed in the middle of the day?" But I was more upset than anyone, and thought that the unbecoming things he had seen must have killed off whatever affection he still had for me.

The weather was cloudy and clear by fits, and spring this year seemed unusually cold. The nights were clear and bright. On the Twelfth came snow driven by a strong wind, and from about noon a quiet rain began to fall. It was a sad but somehow moving day.

I had heard nothing from the Prince since that unfortunate visit. My fears seemed confirmed. But then I remembered that he had four days of penance beginning that day, and I felt a little better. On the Seventeenth my direction was forbidden. A slow rain was falling, and once more the world seemed a sad and gloomy place.

A letter came from a priest I had met at Ishiyama two years before, the one who had gone through the services[16] so solemnly on those sad nights. I had questioned him then and been told that he had come to the temple the year before and was committed to especially ascetic practices.[17] "Well, pray for me then," I remembered answering. He now reported a dream he had had on the night of the Fifth: "You held the sun and the moon in your two hands. The moon you trampled underfoot, but the sun you held to your breast. Perhaps you had better question someone who knows about such things."

The dream seemed a bit wild, and I felt that I would look foolish asking anyone about it. I did chance at the time to meet an interpreter of dreams, however, and I presented this one to him as having concerned a friend of mine. He was astonished. It was a splendid dream, he said. He wanted to know who the person in question was. "Her house will be close to the Emperor and will be able to run the country as it chooses," he explained.

It was as I thought—the interpreter was probably not lying, but the priest who reported the dream was much to be suspected. Such a grand dream could have little bearing on my situation.

Then someone else told me of a dream in which my mansion was seen to have a four-pillar gate.[18] "That means," the sage said, "that someone from your house is to have ministerial rank or very near it.[19] It may be that the Prince is shortly to become a minister, but I prefer to think it refers to your son's future."

Then, a couple of nights ago,[20] I had a dream myself: a man wrote the character for "gate" on my right foot, and I drew back in surprise. This, the dream man said, indicated fine things again about my son's future. I thought it all completely improbable, but still the boy was of such lineage that it was not at all impossible for him to rise to the highest rank,[21] and I thought that the dreams might indeed augur great successes for him.

There were these signs of good fortune, but the future was uncertain. And unhappily I still had but the one child.

For years I had gone about from temple to temple praying for another, but I had exhausted my prayers and was reaching an age where it seemed unlikely that they would be answered. I began to think that I should like to adopt some likely little girl of good rank who could be a companion to the boy and a consolation to him after my death. For some months I asked about for a likely candidate, and finally someone suggested the granddaughter of the late Councilor Kanetada.[22]

"I have heard," my informant said, "that the Prince was at one time keeping company with his daughter, and that she subsequently had a most attractive daughter. If you have no one else in mind, why don't you take that child? She is living with her uncle the priest over at the foot of Mt. Shiga."[23]

Of course—we talked it over and I remembered. There had been some such rumor. While the lady was in mourning for her father (he was descended from the Emperor Yōzei, I believe), the Prince, who had never been able to pass up such an opportunity, did certain favors for her, and the child was the result. Probably it was the merest whim on his part. The lady was well along in years, and she had lived a secluded life. She could hardly have thought that anything serious would develop. But she answered his letters, and he visited her a few times. Then there was some incident about his coming around with a set of her robes—I have forgotten the details. Once he wrote her a poem: "Crossing the barrier and sleeping a hard traveler's sleep[24]—do you think this is but a casual affair for me?" There were other poems, but her replies were quite undistinguished. This was one of them: "It is not for me, this traveler's pillow; I have known no other quite like it, this traveler's sleep." We had a good laugh over that one, with its fuss about travelers' pillows.[25] There seems to have been nothing else particularly noteworthy about the affair. In reply to something or other, she sent this: " 'Night after night the dew wets my sleeves, and even the heat of my thoughts cannot dry them.' " And presently they drifted apart.

Once I had asked him about the affair. "There was indeed a girl born, and she says it is mine. It may well be so," he had replied. "How would it be if you were to take the child in?" This must be the child. I talked the possibility over with my informant and decided that I might well do as the Prince had suggested then. I sent off an intermediary to make inquiries and learned that the child, a stranger to her own father, was now some twelve or thirteen years old. How must the mother have felt, I thought, what laments must have been hers, shut off there with the lake in front and the mountain behind and only the child for company. With my own unhappy experience always on my mind, I felt that I knew how to sympathize with her.

She had a half brother who was a priest near the city.[26] The friend who had first suggested my adopting the child fortunately was acquainted with him and asked him to come for a conference. "I think that would be splendid," he said when he heard our proposal. "They cannot be happy in such a place, and my sister will not live forever, and the child's prospects are most uncertain. They are thinking that it would be best to make her a nun. Indeed they have been preparing her in that temple for some months now."

The next day he crossed the mountains to talk to the child's mother. As they were born of different mothers and had never been particularly close, she was surprised that he had come that distance to see her. After a time he told of his mission. She was choked with tears and could not answer immediately.

Finally controlling herself, she said: "I have resigned myself to living the rest of my days in this lonely place, but it seems tragic that the child should have to be here with me. I do not know what to do—I shall leave it to you to decide."

When he came back the next day and reported all this to me, I was delighted. There must be some tie between the child and me from a previous life, I thought. My friend urged me to write to the lady, and I did so immediately and happily: "Though I have not written to you through all these years, I have heard about your life there, and I should like to think that you have not entirely forgotten me. My request must have seemed a strange one, but when I spoke of my unhappiness to him, your brother the priest was kind enough to transmit my message to you. Now I am delighted to hear that you do not object to my proposal. Though it was not easy to bring the matter up, I had heard of your plans to become a nun,[27] and thought you might perhaps forgive my boldness and consider letting the dear child go.''

The following day I received an answer in which she generously indicated that she was pleased with the idea. She wrote too of the circumstances leading to their conclusion that the child must become a nun, and I felt sad indeed for her. ''My tears flow so that I can hardly see what I write,'' she said, ''and you must find this a strange letter.'' She had cause to weep, I thought.

We exchanged letters twice more and the matter was settled. The priest and others went out to bring the child back to the city, and I thought how hard it must be for them in that lonely temple to see her start off by herself. They could not have done it simply on the impulse of the moment. Perhaps, it occurred to me, they had it in the back of their minds that if she were to come here she would receive the attention to which she was due from her father; and they would be disappointed when they found how little more she saw of him here than out in the country. They might even come to regret having sent her to me. But the agreement was made, and there was no breaking it now.

The Nineteenth seemed to be a propitious day, and I sent my son to bring the child here from the house where she had spent her first days in the city. He rode off in a plain woven-bark carriage[28] with four mounted attendants, a number of footmen, and the friend with whom I had first talked of the child.

Strangely, that day I had a letter from the Prince. ''He is likely to call today,'' I said to the boy, ''and it would not do for him to meet you bringing the girl back. Please get her here as fast as you can. For the time being, at least until we see how things turn out, we had best not say anything to him.''

My precautions did no good, however. The Prince arrived first, and, as I was trying to think of some way to handle the situation, the boy came back. ''What has he been up to?'' the Prince asked. The boy made up all sorts of stories to cover his excursion. I had for some days been afraid that this would happen, and, seeing no other way, I explained that because of my loneliness I was taking in a castaway child.

"Well, now," he replied. "Whose child might it be? Maybe, now that I am getting old, you are throwing me over for some young boy."

I was amused. "Let me show it to you. And perhaps you might make it your child too."

"That I might. Indeed I might. But let's see it, let's see it." And since I was somewhat apprehensive over the child myself, I had her brought in.

She was smaller than I had expected, indeed the merest infant, only about four feet tall. Her hair, which fell to some five inches from the floor, seemed untended, and somewhat rough around the edges as though it had been cut. She was an attractive child, however; her hair and the shape of her head were good, and her appearance generally graceful.

"What a pretty little girl," he said. "Whose child is she?"

And seeing that she was a child of whom we need not be ashamed, I decided to tell him everything. "Well, so you find her attractive?" I said. "Perhaps I shall tell you who she is." I was amused at his impatience. "How annoying you are! Isn't it your own child?"

He was astonished. "But where did you find her, and who is the mother?" And, when I did not come forth immediately with the information, he began guessing. "And then over there beyond the barrier—they say she had a child." I agreed that it might be that child. "How splendid. I have wondered about her. She must have fallen in the world, I have often thought. And to see her for the first time now when she has grown into such a little lady!"

He was overcome with emotion, and the child—who knows what she could have been thinking?—stared at the floor and wept. The rest of us too were deeply moved; it was like something out of an old romance. The Prince pulled out his undersleeve to wipe his eyes time after time.

And then suddenly he was jocular. "I had just about decided to stop coming here," he said, "and now to have a pretty little thing like this turn up. How would it be if she were to go away with me?" And so, laughing and weeping, we talked far into the night.

He called the child to him again early the next morning as he was leaving and found her as attractive as before. "I'll take you with me now," he laughed. "Just climb in when they bring the carriage." And always after that he asked about her in his letters.

Late on the night of the Twenty-fifth there was a fire very near here. I heard that it was at the home of that objectionable woman.[29]

He was in penance on the Twenty-fifth and Twenty-sixth, but he shoved a note for me from under his door. It was friendly, so friendly that it struck me as ironical that our relationship should suddenly have taken this turn after so many years of coolness. The next day my direction was forbidden, but on the following day, the Twenty-eighth, his carriage appeared at about two in the afternoon. It was pulled up into the garden, the blinds raised, and a support put under the shafts, and he climbed out under the red plums, just then in full bloom. He gazed up at them in admiration as he approached; it was a little as though he were in competition with them.

Later it occurred to him that south was forbidden for the following day.[30] "Why didn't you tell me?" he said. "You must have known it all along."

"But what would you have done if I had told you?" I asked.

"I would have gone away, of course." His thoughts seemed to be elsewhere, and since he was so eager to leave us, we all felt that we would do well to keep an eye on him.

"The child must be given lessons in writing and poetry," he told us as he prepared to go that evening. "I think it would be all right for you to take care of it here, but watch that nothing unlooked for happens to her. I think perhaps she and the girl over there[31] should have their coming-out ceremonies together." He went off to the ex-Emperor's.[32] He had to change his direction anyhow, he said, and he might as well get in a visit there.

The cold weather had finally broken. The wind was neither too warm nor too cold, and I felt relaxed and calm. The wind blowing through the plum blossoms seemed to invite the song thrush, the cocks joined in pleasantly, and on the roof the sparrows flitted about building their nests under the tiles. The garden was as though released from a prison of ice.

On the first day of the intercalary Second Month a slow rain fell. The Second and the days following were clear. My direction was open to the Prince on the Third, but I heard nothing. On the Fourth I went to bed still wondering what could explain his silence. Then in the middle of the night there was a great commotion as a fire broke out near-by. I was feeling somewhat listless and did not at first bother to get up. Numbers of people hurried to inquire after me, however, including some who would not ordinarily have come on foot, and I went out to return their greetings. Eventually the fire was brought under control, they all left, and I went back to bed.

Shortly afterwards I heard outrunners approaching and, with surprise, calls of welcome to the Prince. "This place is pitch black," he complained. The lights had been put out. "Apparently she has complete confidence in whoever is with her. I had thought with the fire so near she might be frightened, but maybe I had best go back." But presently he came in and went to bed.

"I have been wanting all evening to come," he said, his manner good-natured and affectionate, "but most of my men had left and I couldn't come without them. Time was when I could jump on a horse and go off where I wanted, but now see how restricted I am. So there I lay, wondering what sort of emergency would give me an excuse to start out as I was, and along came this fire. Strange, isn't it?"

He hurried back early the next morning. His carriage, he said, would look odd in the streets.[33] The Sixth and Seventh he was in penance. The Eighth was rainy, and in the night I could hear the drops beating on the moss of the stones outside.

On the Tenth a friend suggested that we go off quietly together to the Kamo Shrine, and I was quick to accept. I had found the place most revivifying before,[34] and I hoped that this time too it would lift my spirits. But to others the expedition may have seemed a pointless one.[35] As when I had passed before, there were women and children gathering herbs in the marshes at Kitano,[36] with little apparent regard for how they might look, and I thought of the old poem about the marsh grasses and the skirt wet from melting snow.[37] The scenery around Funaoka was most impressive.

It was dark when I reached home, and after I had gone to bed I was again startled by a pounding on the gate, and again, strangely, it was the Prince. I wondered whether he might not have started off to see that woman (the one who lived near here) and been turned away; but he was his usual guileless self. Still I found it impossible to be at ease with him. The sun was fairly high when he left next morning.

The Sixteenth was a dark, rainy day. On the Seventeenth a letter came while we were still in bed: "Your direction is forbidden, and there is nothing we can do about it." But shortly after I had sent an answer he appeared. Perhaps he too thought this evening visit somewhat strange. "I suppose we should offer up something to make amends," he said. He evidently wanted to stay, but I insisted that it would not do, that offerings could not help us, and urged him to leave. Just as he was going out I whispered, "Since this trip has been so unsatisfactory, let's not count tonight among the nights you have come."

"But then all my trouble will have been in vain. We must add at least tonight to the list, whatever we do with the other nights."

There was possibly a good reason for his insistence on being credited with the visit; for the next eight or nine days he stayed away. It was as though he had known that it would be a long time before I would see him again. In the extremity of my gloom, I broke my usual practice and wrote to him without first having had a letter from him: "'Even the sand snipe, clapping its wings endlessly, must cry out for exhaustion as it counts the long nights that alternate with the brief moments I see you.'"

"'What is this?'" he answered. "'My solicitous thoughts quite outnumber the sand snipe's hundred beats; and must she continue to cry out thus despite my efforts?'"

He treated my letter as a joke, and I was sorry I had written.

A sea of cherry petals covered my garden, and from the evening of the Twenty-sixth a rain fell and took away the blossoms that had survived the winds. The Third Month this year was later than usual; already the leaves on the trees were thick enough to hide the sparrows. It was the season when the Kamo Festival would in ordinary years have been held,[38] and I found myself thinking of flutes and sacred branches. But, for all the beauty of the season, I continued to reprove myself for having sent that letter, and I was even more unhappy than usual at his continuing silence. On the Seventh he sent some robes to sew; there was nothing unusual about that, and I acknowledged receipt rather coldly. A quiet rain began to fall from about noon.

On the Tenth there was much excitement at court over the Yawata Festival.[39] I went quietly off to join a relative who was going to the shrine, but returned before dark.[40] The young people indicated strongly that they would like to see the court procession—it would not yet have passed, they said—and I sent them off in the carriage that had just brought me back.

The following day they clamored to see the return procession. I was in bed, not at all well, but I had to acquiesce and four of us started off in a palm-frond carriage.[41] We stopped to the north of the gate to the Reizei-in,[42] where fortunately there were few other spectators, and the child was quite delighted.[43] After a time the procession passed. I saw one of my relatives among the musicians[44] and another among the dancers.

For the rest this was an uneventful period.

On the Eighteenth I went off unobtrusively to the Kiyomizu-dera[45] with some friends. After the early prayers, at about midnight, we went back to the home of one of them, and as we were having something to eat a servant came in to tell us that a fire had broken out to the northwest. Sending someone out to inquire, we were told that it was at Moro-koshi.[46] I was greatly upset, for it seemed to be in the general direction of my house. Then someone came in to say that it was the house of a certain guards officer, and I was thrown quite into a panic. It was separated from mine by only an earthen wall. In what confusion and fright the young people must be, I thought. Without even stopping to put shades on my carriage, I hurried off. By the time I reached home, utterly exhausted, the neighboring mansion was gutted. Mine, however, had been saved, though with great difficulty, and all the people from next door had taken refuge there. I had envisioned the children and all the attendants and serv-ants dashing off on foot in complete confusion, but the boy had loaded them in carriages ready to evacuate and had care-fully barred the gates against robbers. Indeed everything had been handled with the utmost calm and efficiency. I was filled with pride—he was now a man, and he had acted like a man. The refugees from the neighboring estate were mean-while lamenting their misfortune. They had, it seemed, es-caped with nothing more than their lives.

The fire burned down, time passed, and I heard nothing from the Prince. Many others came around to inquire, in-deed some whom I would not have expected to and who would not really have needed to. But not he. I thought of times when he had come flying because there was a fire in the general neighborhood, and I was hurt that he should ignore me now when the fire was next door. I asked the servants and guards whether anyone had told him of the disaster, and everyone I asked reported having done so. How very wretched of him, I thought. And then there was a knocking at the gate, and it was he, and I felt somewhat better.

"I was shocked to hear the news from your men, and I am really very sorry that I did not get here earlier," he said. We went to bed as the cocks were crowing, and the next morning we slept late as though nothing had happened to break the quiet routine.

That day, too, large numbers of people came to ask after me, and the pages sending in names and greetings filled the place with a most disturbing din. "It will get worse and worse," the Prince said, and hurried off.

Sometime later in the day he sent over large stocks of men's clothes, all he could scrape together on short notice, he said. According to his instructions I gave them to the owner of the estate next door for distribution among his household. There was also some hastily cooked rice, a brownish mess that I could scarcely bear to look at. I was told that three of the refugees were ill, and that there had been several quarrels.

From the Twenty-first to the Twenty-fourth the Prince was in penance.

South was a bad direction this year for the people next door,[47] and I knew that they would shortly have to go away. On the Twentieth they all moved to my father's. There I was sure they would be well taken care of and in happier surroundings than here.

I fell back into the old gloom. Again I thought that I would be happy to die. I glanced at the retreat banns[48] fastened to a pillar and wondered if they might suggest to anyone that I was concerned for what might happen to me in this life.

On the Twenty-fifth and Twenty-sixth I was in penance, but on the latter night he came knocking at the gate. I sent to tell him that it was locked because of my retreat, and I heard him go away with almost indecent haste.[49] My direction was forbidden the following day, but still he came and stayed until after dark. Thereafter a series of obstacles prevented his visiting me, another penance here among them.

In the middle of the Fourth Month came the Hollyhock Festival, and I went quietly off with a friend and watched everything from the purification of the vestal. Just as I was about to make an offering at the shrine, the Great Minister from the First Ward[50] arrived for the same purpose. He was most dignified, and his procession grand beyond description. How he resembled the Prince, I thought; the Prince would no doubt be just as impressive in that sort of ceremony. I heard sighs of wonder and admiration around me, and I sank deep into my thoughts.

A friend less prone to melancholy than I took me off on another day to the Chisokuin[51] for more sightseeing. The boy was with us, and as everyone was leaving he noticed a fine lady's carriage[52] after which he started. It dodged off into a crowd, to avoid him perhaps, but he followed and made inquiries. The occupant, it seemed, was a lady from Yamato, and the next day he sent off a poem to her: "My thoughts have turned to you, and I wonder how long a time must pass before our next chance to meet."[53] She sent back that she had no recollection of him, and he tried again: "'My impulsive heart has taken me too far, and I have begun looking for your cedar-lined gate at Mt. Miwa.'"[54] This time she answered: "'You speak of my home at Mt. Miwa; but, cedar-lined though it may be, I cannot tell you where it is for fear of what is wont to happen there.'"[55]

In the Fourth Month I saw nothing of the Prince—he was as scarce as the *unohana*.[56] On the Twenty-cighth a messenger came by with a shrine offering[57] and a letter to the effect that the Prince had not been feeling well.

The Fifth Month came. The child got very excited over the iris roots,[58] and, with nothing else to do, I strung some of them together[59] for her to send over to the child her age at the main house.[60] I attached a poem: "It began its life in a swamp, unobserved; but see how it has put forth its roots."

The lady at the main house sent this back: "'Unobserved it may have been; but the joy of its presentation to the world today is compensation enough.'"

My son, too, put together some iris roots and sent them off to the lady from Yamato with this poem: "Let me dry my sleeves on yours— they are wet from harvesting these roots."

She answered: "'I know nothing of your wet sleeves, and my far from alluring sleeves mean to have as little knowledge of their drying.'"

Rain fell for about three days running from early on the

Sixth, and I heard that the river had overflowed and that numbers of people had been drowned. I had sad thoughts about that and about many other things, but I was no longer concerned with the possibility of any improvement in my relations with the Prince.

I received a letter from that priest at Ishiyama saying that he was praying for me. "I have no more ambitions for myself," I answered, "and what have I then to expect from the Buddha? But pray instead that my son may grow into a decent and respected gentleman." But in spite of my professed resignation, I found my eyes clouding over as I wrote.

On the Tenth the boy delivered a letter from his father: "I have not been feeling well, and I am afraid I have neglected you shamefully. How have you been?"

I waited to send an answer back with the boy the following day: "I thought of answering your letter immediately last night, but somehow I felt that it would not be right unless I had it delivered through my son. You ask how I am. Well, I am at length resigned to the fact that I cannot shape things to my will, and I am feeling rather content. Might it seem unkind if I were to refer you to the poem about how one doesn't mind the wait as long as the wind isn't cold?"[61]

In the evening the boy came back. He had not seen his father and not been able to get an answer. The Prince, it seemed, was off at the Kamo springs.[62] "Isn't that splendid?" I murmured automatically.

The weather was stormy and violent, and now and then my thoughts turned to the farmers who had to be out in the fields. I had not yet heard a cuckoo. I was sleeping too well. Cuckoos are for people who have worries and can lie awake listening. "I heard it last night," or, "Just at dawn it sang," my people would say, and I was ashamed that only I seemed to have missed it. "'And have I slept so well?'" I said to myself, hoping no one would notice. "'No—quite the opposite—my sad thoughts have made them hear a cuckoo yet more plaintive.'"

The rest of the month was dull, and the hot weather came with the Sixth Month. Once when the east side of the house was unbearably warm I went out to the south veranda. The cicadas were droning heavily outside. I thought I heard someone coming, and, as I leaned back out of sight for him to pass, I noticed an old man standing under the trees with a rake in his hand. He was somewhat deaf and apparently had not yet noticed the insects, but a particularly loud humming caught his attention. "'Yoi-zo, yoi-zo,' you go, you big crickets,"[63] he said, looking up in surprise. "Even you know what season it is." And the cicadas went on humming as though in assent—"So, so, so."[64] How interesting and yet how sad it must have seemed to him, this passing of the seasons. I was struck with the sadness of it myself.

My son broke off a branch of brocade tree,[65] splashed with red even then, and sent it off to the lady from Yamato with this poem: "The dew lies heavy under the summer trees, and already the leaves have turned for sorrow."

She answered: "'The dew has turned the leaves, you say; and are your solemn words as easily colored?'"

That evening I had a long and friendly letter from the Prince, something of a surprise, coming as it did after a silence of more than twenty days. I had grown used both to his inattentiveness and to his unpredictability, which I see no point in discussing. Yet when, on such occasions, I found him somewhat kinder, I was touched as well as annoyed. Perhaps he too was sad, and growing old. I was quicker than usual with my answer.[66]

Since my father's place was at the time undergoing repairs,[67] he and his household moved in with me. My house was quite alive with them, and the days went noisily by. But I heard nothing from the Prince. His silence was such that I wondered what my guests must think of it. Toward the middle of the month they all moved back again, and the customary dullness reasserted itself here. With the approach of the Festival of the Dead, my people lamented the inadequacy of our equipment, but on the Fourteenth the usual supplies arrived with an inventory from the Prince's steward.[68] I wondered how long even these perfunctory favors would go on.

The First of the Eighth Month was rainy with sudden, autumn-like showers. Toward the middle of the afternoon it cleared, and the autumn cicadas[69] took up their humming. "Noisy insects, singing in the grass"—I thought of the well-known verse—"what sorrow makes you cry out so when I bear mine in silence?"[70] This was a strange and sad time for me. The month before, I had had a sign that I was to die this month, and I wondered whether the time might be approaching. I listened without interest to talk of preparations for the wrestling meet.[71] On the Eleventh, I had an extremely odd dream. The interpretation unfortunately was quite incredible. . . .[72] I said nothing. "Why are you so quiet?" he asked.

"What is there to say?" I replied.

"Well, you might ask me why I haven't come to see you, why I haven't asked after you; you might tell me how wicked and mean I have been, you might beat me and pinch me."

"Indeed, you have said all there is to say," I replied and again lapsed into silence. Early the next morning he left; he would come again after the banquet for the wrestling meet, he said, but until then he would be busy with preparations. The banquet was held on the Seventeenth, I heard, and the end of the month came with still no word from him. I knew, of course, that his duties could no longer be pressing, but as his silence was in no sense novel, I thought little of it. Instead I was filled with sadness and apprehension as the time indicated by that omen approached.

The boy continued sending letters to the lady from Yamato. The answers appeared to be written by someone else, and finally in annoyance he sent this verse: "I look into the corners of the room in the evening, and see the spider spinning his own web; can you not do as well?"

I do not know what she had in mind, but she sent this written on pure white paper with some pointed object: "'Knowing how fragile a thing it is before the winds that blow, how am I to trust to the spider's web?'"

He sent again: "'If the spider is to trust even a little to the fine line of its web, then must it not have someone to protect if from those blasts?'"

She said it had grown too dark for an answer. The next morning, perhaps thinking of that letter on white paper, he sent off this: " 'The swan's tracks have disappeared, and the sands of Shirahama in Tajima are as blank as the snow their name suggests.' "[73]

This time she said she had to be off somewhere and did not answer; and when the next day he asked by word of mouth whether she was back and pressed her for an answer, she sent back: "How can I answer such a poem? It is really too old-fashioned."

And he replied: "You are quite right. 'With the time I have spent in silent lamenting I have grown as old and musty as the God of Furu.' "[74]

She said she was in penance and would be the following day too. Early on the day it appeared the penance would have ended, he sent this: " 'I glimpsed her as in a dream; and now, bewildered, I wait for the nun's door to open.' "

This time, too, she turned the messenger away with excuses, and the boy sent off this: " 'You have practiced at Mt. Katsuragi[75] and become like the One-Word God.' Who has taught you to behave thus?"

Young people will say hotheaded things.

I took to painting pictures during these long autumn nights (the spring nights were no better). It was a fair alternative, I thought, to my constant brooding, and I might leave something behind for people to remember me by. Day after day I waited for the fatal moment, but the month passed, and the Ninth Month too, and nothing happened. It was just as I had always thought: the happy are sooner released from this life than the wretched.

On the night of the Twenty-seventh or Twenty-eighth of the Ninth Month, when I was away from home to avoid transgressing on the Hearth God,[76] I was informed that the Prince had arrived at my empty house. I was not particularly interested and dismissed the messenger with a nod of acknowledgment.

The Tenth Month, it seemed to me, was rainier than usual. Toward the middle of the month, I went off at the invitation of some friends to pray and enjoy the autumn leaves at the usual temple in the western mountains. It was alternately rainy and clear, and the mountain scenery the whole day was moving and impressive.

On the First of the Eleventh Month the Great Minister from the First Ward[77] died, and that night, as we were lamenting the event, eight or nine inches of snow fell, the first of the year. I thought of his unfortunate children having to go through the funeral in such unpleasant weather. I had a great deal of leisure for such thoughts.

With each new administration the Prince seemed to prosper.[78] I saw him on about the Twentieth of the Twelfth Month.

✳ *The First Year of Ten-en* (973)

THE USUAL festivities covered the first days of the new year, but I was conscious only of growing older. It was pleasant, though, to hear the song of the first thrush. On about the Fifth the Prince came during the daytime, and on about the Tenth and again on about the Twentieth after we were all undressed and in bed. It was a strange month indeed that saw so many visits, especially since, with the annual lists of appointments and honors, it was such a busy month at court.

The Second Month came, and the red plums were redder and brighter than usual; but there was no one to enjoy them with me. The boy did break off a branch and send it to the lady from Yamato with this poem: "As I wait and wait the long years through, my tears stain my sleeves the bloody color of these flowers."

"'What fickleness is this,'" she answered, "'letting the flowers change one's color, and waiting under them without invitation?'"

We wondered if that was all we could expect from her.[79]

The Prince appeared at about noon on the Third. I felt old and worn and ashamed to have him see me. After a while he remembered that my direction was forbidden and prepared to leave. He was dressed beautifully in a white robe with a lavender lining, most intricately woven and so elegant that it was hard to believe that I had managed the dyeing, and glossed trousers with a modest receding pattern.[80] As I heard his outrunners clearing the way in the distance, I thought how wilted and rumpled I must have looked by comparison. I glanced at myself in the mirror. This time surely I had succeeded in strangling any affection that might have survived, I thought. I could not take my mind off the incident. When from the first of the month rainy days succeeded one another, it was exactly as though my laments "were putting out new shoots" in the rain.[81]

Late on the night of the Fifth there was another bit of excitement: that woman's[82] house caught fire again. This time it was completely destroyed.

On about the Tenth, toward noon, I saw the Prince. He was going away on a pilgrimage to Kasuga,[83] he said, and (odd remark) he regretted that the trip must keep us apart.

Practice for the archery meet at the Reizei-in[84] began from the middle of the Second Month. The boy was chosen for one of the teams, and we were kept busy helping him get ready. This year there were very large numbers of high officials[85] present. The boy selected his arrows and set out, but I was not sanguine—he had been somewhat offhand in his preparation. Yet the reports were favorable: the boy himself shot first and hit the mark twice, and his colleagues, riding on the momentum, one after another scored good shots; and the team walked off with the day's prize. The boy was still talking of it days later. "Those last shots were really a delight," he said, and I am sure I felt even more pleased than he.

Then came the bustle for the Yawata Festival.[86] With nothing else to do, I set off quietly to watch. An elaborate procession with a noisy gang of outrunners approached, and I recognized the Prince's men, and then the Prince himself, riding with his blinds up, quite in the public eye. I was conscious of what a poor figure I must put up by contrast. He looked my way, but ducked behind his fan as he passed.

The next day I had a letter from him, and at the end of my answer I wrote, "Everyone agrees that you put on a most extravagant show yesterday. But why did you hide your face? Most kittenish of you."

"It was hardly 'kittenish,' " he came back. "On the contrary, I did it out of shame for my wrinkles. And it was certainly unkind of them to call my procession 'extravagant.' "

The Tenth of the Third Month passed, and still I heard nothing from him. As this was a longer silence than there had been for some time, I wondered if I had at length had my last letter.

The boy meanwhile was keeping up his correspondence with the lady from Yamato. His own letters, he was afraid, were lacking in appropriate imagery and had a rather childish ring, and he had me too compose poems for her. There was this, for instance: "It has to now been hidden by the water; but one may wonder whether the iris will perhaps consent to be pulled." And this was her answer, uninteresting enough: " 'It is but a poor swamp grass not worth your trouble, whatever may be your plans for bringing it out.' "

On about the Twentieth I saw the Prince. On the Twenty-third or Twenty-fourth a fire broke out near-by and spread until evening.[87] The Prince appeared immediately but left when he saw that my house was safe. "We gain a bit of face from having them know he is here, and has come to make inquiries," I heard my people say, and no doubt I did seem to them to have reached a point where a perfunctory visit made such a difference.

On the last day of the month he came again. "This is quite a lively spot when you have fires," he remarked as he came in.

"Ah, but 'my thoughts, like the watch fires, blaze up every night,' "[88] I replied.

Early in the Fifth Month the boy sent this to the lady from Yamato: " 'Perhaps we may have a friendly song from you too, now that the time has come when the cuckoo can no longer restrain himself.' "

She replied with this: " 'When the cuckoo sings thus without inhibition, is it not a sign that he is about to return to the wilds?' "

This one of the boy's was dated the Fifth:[89] " 'The day of the iris comes again, to tell me how long I have waited.' "

Her reply: "'I really cannot say how many days of the iris may have come and gone. I only know that this one too will go.'"[90]

We wondered what could be making her so peevish.

I continued throughout the month to have occasional fits of depression.

On about the Twentieth I had a letter from the Prince, attached to a food bag.[91] He planned to give the bag, he said, to someone starting off on a long journey, and he wanted me to sew a lining. Another letter was delivered as I was finishing the work: "How are you coming? While you are about it, why don't you fill the bag with poems? I have not been feeling well enough to think up any myself."

I was greatly amused. "I shall give you all the poems you want. But perhaps you had better send another bag, lest the poems overflow the first one."

"I have not been feeling at all well," he said a couple of days later, "but I thought too much time was going by and, as a last resort, wrote those poems myself. Here they are, and here are the answers I got back. Let me know which ones you think best."

It was a rainy day, and I fell rather into the spirit of the thing. Though I had some ideas on the poems, I thought it would be rather presumptuous of me to undertake a critical essay. Instead, I sent back a poem of my own: "The east wind, strong and willing, blows poems this way; the answering wind I am afraid is less effective."[92]

I saw him about as usual during the Sixth and Seventh Months. On the Twenty-eighth of the Seventh Month he announced that he had left the wrestling meet early to call on me. He did not come again until the end of the Eighth Month. I heard that he was still seeing that woman. I concluded that his affections had shifted for good.

My house was going to ruin, and I felt increasingly distraught. My father[93] suggested that it would be best to let it out, since my retinue was a small one, and move into his place on the Nakagawa.[94] I had spoken to the Prince many times of the possibility that I might move, but now that the time approached I felt that I should let him know I was finally leaving. I sent to tell him that I wanted to talk to him, but he replied coldly that he was in penance. "If that is how he feels," I said to myself, "very well," and I went ahead with the moving.

The new place fronted on the river, near the mountains. I found it rather satisfying to think that I was there by my own choice.[95]

The Prince apparently did not hear for two or three days that I had moved. Then, on the Twenty-fifth or Twenty-sixth, I had a letter complaining that I had not informed him.

"I did think of telling you," I answered, "but this is such a poor place that I assumed you would not want to visit it. I had hoped to see you once more where we used to meet."

I spoke as though I considered our separation final, and he seemed to agree: "You are perhaps right. It might not be easy for me to visit you there." And I heard no more.

The Ninth Month came. Looking out early one morning after the shutters were raised, I saw that a mist had come in over the garden from the river[96] so that only the summits of the mountains to the east were visible. Somehow it seemed to shut me in from the world, alone. "'I had hoped that it would go on flowing, this Nakagawa,'" I said to myself, "'but it seems to have wasted away.'"[97]

The fields to the east were being cut, and in long rows the straw hung drying. When, rarely, a visitor came, we would send someone out to get feed for the horses, or to bring in some new rice for roasting.[98] Now and then the boy took his hawks out to try their wings in the open.

He seems to have sent this to the lady he was courting: "'Am I to spend my whole life alternately despairing and hoping, fearing for the thin thread that should bind us?'"[99]

There was no answer. Later he sent this: "'Who is your companion these long hard nights that I must spend alone, my sleeves drenched with the dew?'"

This time there was an answer, but it does not seem worth putting down.

The Prince maintained his silence, though at the end of

the Ninth Month I was favored with some winter clothes to sew. There was a letter, the messenger said, but he had lost it.

"It will not be good for you if he finds out," I told the fellow. "Let us say that I sent no answer." I never learned what was in the letter, and I sent the finished clothes back without a word.

With that, even the road to love through dreams was blocked. I heard nothing from him until, at the end of the year, he sent some under-robes to be done, and not even a note with them. I was annoyed and hesitated to take them, but my people urged me to give him one more chance. "Let us see what happens," they said. "It may be that he has been put off by your coldness." And so I had them carefully tailored and sent them back with my son on New Year's Day.

"He thought you did them very nicely," the boy reported, but there was no letter. I was most annoyed.

My father had had a new child in the Eleventh Month.[100] For some reason I had not made a congratulatory call, and I thought that, with the new year, I ought at least to send some sort of present (I could arrange nothing elaborate of course). I attached a branch of plum blossoms to the usual sort of thing, a white baby's dress, and had it delivered, with this poem, by the Chief of the Crown Prince's Guard:[101] "We have been shut in by the snow this long winter, but now we see the plum blossoms along the hedge."[102]

The man delivered it in the evening and came back the following morning with a light-purple under-robe and this poem: "The tender branch blooming among the gusts of snow has grown more fragrant with your asking after it."

Such duties occupied my time, and the celebrations for the new year passed.

Someone invited me to go along on a quiet pilgrimage, and I saw no reason for refusing. The place was crowded when we arrived. It was most unlikely, of course, that anyone would recognize me, but somehow I felt uncomfortable and exposed. Great clusters of icicles hung from the eaves of the purification hall, and, as we were admiring them and preparing to leave, a rather eccentric figure went by munch-

ing on a piece of ice. At first I took him to be someone of
rank, though he was dressed in children's clothes and wore
his long hair done up in a strange bundle. He seemed to have
a reserve supply of ice in his sleeve.

"Are you speaking to me?" he asked, bowing, as my
friend questioned him. His mouth was stuffed with ice, and
I could see that, contrary to my first impression, he was a
commoner. "Why, unless you eat ice, you won't get your
prayers answered."

What an inauspicious thing, I thought—it amounted to
wetting your sleeves gratuitously. And I recited to myself
a verse: "The ice that chills my sleeves knows no spring;
and yet there are those who can go about with the spring in
their hearts."

Three days later, in a driving snowstorm, I went on a pilgrimage to Kamo. I had a bad cold in the Tenth Month and
felt vaguely unwell for the rest of the year.[103]

✳ *The Second Year of Ten-en (974)*

THE NEW YEAR came, and on the Fifteenth the boy's
men lit ceremonial fires to chase out the devils.[104] They
made rather a party of it well on into the night. "Quiet
down a bit," someone shouted, and I went to the edge of the
room for a look. The moon was bright, and the mountains
to the east shone dim and icy through the mist. Leaning
quietly against a pillar, I thought about myself and my loneliness, how I should like to go off to a mountain temple
"away from this torment"[105] if only I could, and how I had
not seen him for five months, not since the end of the summer. I could not keep back my tears. "'I would join my
song with the song thrush,'" I whispered to myself, "'but
the thrush has forgotten the new year.'"

From about the middle of the month a campaign was
launched to get the boy an official position. He was, I heard,
in close competition[106] with someone or other, and the out-
come was in considerable doubt. Toward the end of the
month, a surprise letter came from the Prince announcing
that the boy had been made Vice-Chief of the Right Sta-

bles.[107] There followed a round of courtesy calls, including one on the Kami, the head of the boy's new office—his uncle,[108] as it happened. The visit was a pleasant one, the boy reported, and in the course of the conversation the Kami asked about the girl here, what sort of child she was, how old she was, and all. I put little significance in the questions. The child was obviously not old enough to be considered for marriage.

Meanwhile practice for the archery meet at the Reizei-in had begun. My son and the Kami were on the same team and saw each other frequently, and each time they met, the Kami repeated his inquiries about the child. I began to wonder what he might have in mind.

On about the Twentieth of the Second Month I had a dream. . . .[109]

We set out quietly. It was not far, but still rather deep in the mountains.[110] The dead grass had been burnt away, and the flowers were late; it would have been an impressive road had they been out. The way was quiet, without even the song of a thrush, for in the deep mountains the birds are still.[111] Only the water boiled and churned through the valley.

I was quite wretched. There must be people free from these torments, I thought, from the uncontrollable restlessness that continued to drive me off to the mountains.

We arrived as the vesper bells were ringing. I had votive candles lighted and went through the night services,[112] still feeling miserably unhappy. Toward dawn rain began to fall. We went down to the priests' quarters in the gathering daylight and debated what to do, and presently my men went off in search of raincoats and umbrellas.[113] Left to myself, I looked out over the valley. Clouds were rising slowly, a most melancholy sight. "'Who could have known that I would one day be parting the mountain clouds with my sleeves?'" I said to myself.

A heavy rain was falling by the time we were ready to start, but we could wait no longer. I walked off with the little girl beside me. Her discomfort seemed to add to mine, but somehow we arrived back.

The following evening the boy rested awhile after archery practice[114] and then came in to see me. "My father," he said, "mentioned that since last year the Kami has frequently asked about the girl here, and he said that he himself wondered how she was getting along, whether she had grown and whether she was developing into the right sort of young lady. Afterwards the Kami asked whether my father had said anything, and I answered that he had. Then he said that day after tomorrow is a lucky day and he would like to send his first letter here then."

How very strange, I thought as I went to sleep; the girl was surely not old enough for such attentions.

On the day indicated came a letter, one whose contents demanded the greatest caution: "For some months I have had the problem on my mind; and when I asked someone to approach the Prince, I was told that he had been informed of the substance of my proposal and had suggested that I write immediately to you. But still I hesitated lest you think it strange and presumptuous of me. Then, too, I have had no good channel whereby to approach you, but now that your son has been put in my department I think I could visit your house without stirring up any rumors." All this he said as though it were the most natural thing in the world. "Let me go first to Musashi's,"[115] he added.

This required an answer, but first I sent for the Prince's views. "He is in penance," said the messenger, "and for that and various other reasons I was not able to show him your letter."

Five or six days went by, and the Kami, perhaps getting impatient, sent to say that there was an urgent matter on which he must see the boy. The latter sent back with a promise to come immediately, but before he could start, it began to rain. Feeling sorry for the Kami, he was making his preparations when the messenger brought another note. It was written on thin red paper and attached to a spray of red plum: "The Isonokami is not usually considered enough to make people break promises, you know.[116] 'This branch of flowers is damp with the spring rain, but with secret tears my sleeves are damper still.' My boy, my boy, will you not come to see me?'' For some reason the last words had been inked out.

The boy was wondering what sort of answer to make, but I thought all these letters a nuisance and told him to say that he had met the messenger on the road.

When he came back he said that the Kami was most annoyed at us for not having sent at least an interim reply while we waited for something from the Prince.

Two or three days later the Prince finally read my letter. ''He said that he did not understand why we were hesitating so,'' the boy reported, ''that we could easily think of an answer to put my uncle off, and that he himself had told my uncle that he would give a definite answer after he had thought the idea over. He said too that it would not be a good idea for my uncle to be coming here before things were settled. There are not many people who know that the girl is here, and it might seem strange for a young man to be calling on you.'' I was most annoyed, for it was as if he were confirming the rumors.[117]

That day I sent off my answer to the Kami: ''I thought at first that I owed your unexpected letter to the boy's having been appointed to your office, and I of course intended to answer immediately. That strange business about the Prince puzzled me, however, and it has taken as long to get an answer from him as it would have to send an embassy to China. Unfortunately, his answer has been vague; there is little I can say to encourage you.'' At the end I added: ''This Musashi whose room you speak of borrowing: she asks me to inform you that she does not permit visits from just anyone.''

There were other letters. I did not answer them all, and even when I did I shuddered at the rumors I might be starting.

The Third Month came. The Kami also wrote to the Prince, it seemed, through a suitable lady in waiting, and he sent me a note enclosing her reply. ''His Highness seems to have trouble making up his mind,'' said the note. This was the enclosure: ''His Highness, shuffling through the calen-

dar, says that this month is unlucky, but that next month
might be better.''

How quick he is with his calendar, I thought; but the
whole thing is impossible. The woman must have made it up.

On about the Seventh or Eighth of the Third Month the
Kami was announced. ''What a nuisance he is! Tell him I
am out,'' I ordered. ''He will want to talk about the child,
and really it is much too early.''

He came into the garden and stood there just behind the
lattice fence. There was nothing particularly remarkable
about his dress—a soft informal cloak,[118] well glossed, and a
sword. Yet he would have been a handsome figure under any
circumstances, and as he stood there toying with a slightly
frayed red fan, the wind blowing at the netting of his cap,[119]
he was as dashing as a hero in a picture. My women soon
heard that a handsome man had come, and out they hurried,
wrinkled and undressed, for a look at him. Just as they had
all collected for the fun, a gust of wind caught up the shade
in front of them, whipping it wildly in and out. In the greatest consternation they fluttered about trying to hold it
down, but still he must have seen them. Since they were
hardly a pleasing sight, it was most embarrassing.

This all happened while we were waiting for my son, who
had returned late the night before from archery practice and
was still asleep, to come and advise the gentleman that I was
away. Eventually he appeared and delivered the message,
and, since the shutters had been lowered against the wind,[120]
the excuse was a plausible enough one.

Still the Kami insisted on coming up on the veranda.
''Bring me a mat,''[121] he said. ''This is such a lucky day that
I must trouble you for a few moments.'' He talked briefly
with the boy and went off lamenting his misfortune in having
found us away.

Two days later I sent by word of mouth an apology for
not having been here to receive him. ''It was indeed unfortunate,'' he answered (indeed more than once), ''but I
should like to come again.'' I protested that that would be
most improper and could only give rise to rumors. My

words could hardly have been called an invitation. He indicated that he would like to talk to the boy, however, and one evening we heard that he was on his way.

There seemed to be no help for it. I had a couple of shutters raised and a light brought to the veranda and made preparations to receive him just inside.[122] The boy went out to invite him in. He started through the side door, then hesitated and asked first to have his respects brought in to me. I acknowledged them and invited him inside, and after a moment of subdued laughter I heard the rustle of his clothing, properly restrained, as he approached.

The conversation, in subdued voices, was punctuated now and then by the click of fan against baton.[123] I did not join in. "Please tell your mother," he essayed presently, "how sorry I am about my visit the other day."

The message was relayed to me, and the boy pressed me for an answer. I approached the curtain on my knees. He was silent for a time, and I felt still more constrained to silence. Then, thinking that he perhaps was not sure I was there, I coughed encouragingly. With that he began: "It was unfortunate that you should have been away." And he poured out everything, from first to last, that had to do with his suit.

"But really this is a most inappropriate time to be suggesting such a thing," I replied. "What you say is entirely wild. The child is far from ready for marriage. She is not small, she is tiny—hardly yet the size of a young mouse." I was most uncomfortable, and my voice seemed affected even to me. Outside in the rain[124] frogs croaked noisily.

"This is such a lonesome and fearful place," I began again, "that even we inside the house are hardly comfortable." It was by then quite dark.

"You must not be frightened," he answered. "Tell yourself that I am here to take care of you." It grew still later. "And then the boy here will soon be busy getting ready for the festival,[125] and I can help with that too. I shall tell my brother of this talk, and I shall come again in a day or two to let you know what he says."

He made gestures toward leaving, and I peeked through a tear in the curtain for a better look at him. The light on the

veranda, I saw, had gone out. Because of the discreetly
shaded light inside the curtain, I had not noticed. Thus he
must have been able to see me. "How wretched of you not
to tell me," I burst out. He hurried off without a word of
explanation. [126]

The first visit thus accomplished, he came repeatedly. His
request was always the same. I had decided that if he received
the Prince's permission I would have to acquiesce, though
reluctantly. "But I already have the Prince's consent," he
insisted noisily. "He has given his consent, and he has even
suggested a day late this month as a lucky one for the wedding."

But fortunately the Hollyhock Festival was approaching
and the Kami had to restrain himself while we got my son
ready. He was to represent his office. As it happened, however, our labors came to nothing. The boy saw a dead dog on
the day of the purification[127] and had to stay at home after all.

The Kami took up the pursuit again. "Why don't you ask
the Prince about it if you don't believe me?" he persisted.
"Tell him I have told you what he said."[128]

I could not imagine that the Prince was indeed giving different stories to the two of us, and I concluded that I had
better send for a written statement with which to counter
this new pressure from the Kami.

"I had thought to give my permission," the Prince wrote,
"but with the confusion of the festival and all, things have
dragged on so that I think we had better put it off. If he hasn't
changed his mind by the Eighth Month, you might tell him,
perhaps we can arrange something."

I was vastly relieved. "This is what he says," I wrote.
"And indeed haven't I said all along that you were being
much too hasty, riffling through your calendar?"

There was no answer from the Kami for a time, and then
he appeared in person. "I have come to tell you how extremely annoyed I am," he sent in through a messenger.

"What fearsome things you say. But come in," I sent
back.

He was indeed angry. "I have been coming here day and
night for a good while now. And you only draw things out."

He talked to the boy for a time, and as he was about to leave he asked for an inkstone, wrote a short note, and, knotting it closed, thrust it in at me. Thereupon he stalked out. "'What of the promised Fourth Month?'" his note said. "'The cuckoo has deserted a most forlorn person.' I cannot tell you how dejected I am. I shall come again in the evening." His handwriting quite shamed my own. I wrote an answering poem and had it sent after him as he left. "You must control yourself. The Fourth Month has passed, and the hollyhocks; but the citrons will put out their flowers."[129]

On the Twenty-second, the day he said the Prince had chosen for the wedding, the Kami appeared again. He was cooler and more collected than before, and his stubbornness was particularly trying. "And so the Prince's promise has come to nothing," he complained, "and I am to be kept waiting. Can't you try to understand how I feel—can't you do something?"

"How can you persist in that sort of talk?" I answered. "You complain of having to wait, but perhaps while you are waiting the child will reach adolescence."

"It doesn't matter how much of a child she is. I can still talk to her, can't I?"

"She is at an age when even that is impossible." But my arguments appeared to have little effect. His face wore a tragic expression.

"My heart is pounding furiously. At least let me inside the curtain, and then I will go away. I will be happy if I am allowed to work up to my objective step by step."[130]

He laid his hand on the curtain.[131] Deeply alarmed, I pretended not to have heard what he said. "It is getting very late—the time of night, I suppose, when you are accustomed to having such ideas."

"I expected you to be a little more friendly. I would be so terribly happy if you could give me some encouragement. I have been waiting so long.[132] But I have behaved badly. I do not blame you if you are annoyed." He stepped back, apologizing profusely.

I could not help feeling sorry for him. "Please try to be-

have as you would at court, or at the old Emperor's.[133]
Really, you have been most impulsive.''

''What a painful suggestion that is!'' And suddenly he
came in behind the curtain as he had threatened.[134] I could
think of nothing to say. ''Well, I have offended you,'' he
finally burst out. ''You will not be bothered any more until
I hear you are ready with your permission. You are quite
right. I am sorry.'' And after a time he went out, snapping
his fingers in exasperation. Someone tried to give him a
torch, but he refused it and went home in the dark.

I sent to ask after him early the next morning. ''How sad
it must have been, going home without torch. I have been
worried about you.

    Dark must that mountain road have been. And when—
    He would not say—will the cuckoo come again?''

The messenger did not wait for an answer, but soon one
was delivered: ''You must forgive me for last night.

    Abashed in the morning sun he is. How then
    Can your cuckoo say when he will come again?''

But despite his fit of temper, he appeared at my gate the
next day. My son, he said, had a great many calls to make
that day, and he thought it would be best for them to go first
to the office together. Again he asked for an inkstone, which
I sent out with paper. He left rather a long letter in a
strangely shaky hand: ''What sins from previous lives might
be responsible for the way in which my love is blocked?
Matters grow worse and worse, and I begin to wonder
whether the marriage will ever take place. But I shall bother
you no more. I am thinking of withdrawing to a mountain
temple somewhere.''

''What a frightening letter,'' I replied. ''I find it hard to
know what you are talking about, for the source of your dissatisfaction is not here. I am not the one to complain to. I
know little about mountains, but perhaps I could help with
a valley.''

The two of them rode off together, and the boy came back
later on a fine horse he had been given to use.

That evening the Kami came again. ''I have regretted very
much my behavior of the other night,'' he said, ''and the

more I have thought about it the worse I have felt. But I have come today a different man to tell you that from now on I shall behave like a gentleman and simply wait for some word from the girl's father. You have been kind enough to dissuade me from suicide;[135] really, though, a thousand years can give me no happiness if I have to go on like this. Counting the months over on my fingers, I see that I have somehow gone through three of them; but the ones that lie ahead seem very long indeed. I hope you won't mind, in the unhappy weeks to come, if now and then I stop by and pay my respects like your humblest servant." There had been a distinct change in his manner, and he spoke with remarkable glibness.

I answered in what I hoped was a similar manner, and he left early.

The boy continued to be called in for conferences, and once he came back with some Japanese paintings[136] of the Kami's. One showed a woman leaning on the railing of what looked to be the fishing pavilion[137] of a mansion; sunk in thought, she gazed out at the island in the garden lake. I pasted a verse to it: "What are we to do when the waves of the lake surge up over the waiting heart?"[138]

The other was of a man, a bachelor probably, who had started a letter and who was sitting, chin in hand, apparently sunk in thought. For this one I wrote: "'These letters no doubt are off to numerous romantic addresses, even as the strands of the spider's web blow in all directions.'"

I returned the pictures with the poems attached.

The Kami continued to bother me, urging me to press for the Prince's permission, and I decided that I would again have to have something to show him from the Prince. "He keeps up his attack, and I have run out of things to say to him," I wrote.

"We have made it clear when he can expect an answer, and I do not understand why he should continue to visit you," the Prince replied. "In fact it is rather widely rumored that, pending the time we have set, you are being more considerate than is necessary. I should like to have you know that I am not pleased."

At first I thought he must be joking, but several more notes came, all indicating that he really was jealous. Astonished, I sent off a protest: "It is not by my choice that he continues his visits. I have told him repeatedly that I am not the one he should appeal to. I really must protest against your extraordinary accusations. 'What young pony could be tempted by these withered autumn grasses?'[139] Your letters quite fill me with confusion."

Through the rest of the month, the Kami continued to plead his case. This year the cuckoos were remarkably clear, almost as though they were singing in the rafters,[140] and at the end of one of his letters he wrote, "One can hardly rest for the extraordinary sound of these cuckoos."[141] His tone was most respectful, without a suggestion of improper intentions. "Tell your son, please, that unless things go better, presently there will be no feed bucket,"[142] he also remarked in his letter. The boy had borrowed a feed bucket from him some time before.

"We hadn't realized that you had set conditions," I answered. "Perhaps it was a mistake for us to become involved with that bucket."

And he immediately came back: "Indeed there were conditions, and I should like to see that bucket where it belongs in the next day or so."

The end of the month came, and, perhaps because his interest had been dulled by the slowness of the affair, the Kami stayed away for a time. On the Fourth of the Fifth Month, a very rainy day, he asked the boy to come calling if there was a break in the rain. "Tell your mother," he said in his note, "that my sad fate has become clear to me and that I have nothing more to say to her." It appeared that he had no real business, and after some light banter the boy was allowed to come home.

It was decided that the little girl[143] was to go on a pilgrimage that day, rain and all, and I saw no reason why I should not go along. At the suggestion of one of my women I had three dolls' dresses made of fine, stiff cloth[144] for her to take as offerings. To the skirt of each I attached a verse—the goddess no doubt knows what I had in mind:

"I offer this pure white robe; may we see again a relationship as close as that of old."

"I fold back the skirt of this Chinese robe. Would I could find as pliant one whom I knew of old."

"I offer the goddess this plain summer robe, and the unchanging prayer that goes with it is as simple."

My brother appeared before we had raised the shutters on the morning of the Iris Festival.[145] "What's this—you haven't put out the irises yet?[146] You really should have done it last night."

We got up in great excitement and prepared to open the house. "Leave the shutters down for a while," he said. "The scent will drift in, and then you can have a good long look." But we were all up and helping him.

It was a fine morning. The wind had changed and the sky had cleared, and the scent of the iris roots spread quickly through the house. Out on the veranda the boy and my brother had gathered all sorts of plants and were busy with medicine packets.[147] We were rather alarmed at a flock of cuckoos—there really were too many of them this year—near the toilet; it was a bad omen surely.[148] But when two and three flew off singing into the sky the effect was pure delight. "The mountain cuckoo on the day of the iris,"[149] someone murmured, and all of us took it up, one after another.

Later in the morning a message came from the Kami suggesting that my son go with him to watch the mounted archery. The boy agreed, but several more messengers came to urge him along before he finally left the house.

Early the next morning another letter came (we did not see the Kami himself): "There was so much excitement yesterday that I was not able to talk to you. If you have time today, though, please come around. I am still most distressed by your mother's coldness. If I live long enough, perhaps I shall win her over. And if I die, all my worry will have gained me nothing. But I have talked too much. Keep this letter to yourself."

Another letter came two days later. Again he had something to talk over—could the boy come to see him or should he come here? I sent the boy off immediately. The last thing in the world I wanted was for the Kami to come here. As usual, the Kami had nothing in particular to say.

About two days later, early in the morning, the boy was summoned again. There was a message to be passed on to me, it seemed. Before he could leave the house, however, a heavy rain began to fall. It continued all day, and finally toward evening he sent a note of apology: "I languish in the rain that has prevented my visiting you. 'Our visits have been as steady as the waters of this Nakagawa. How sad it must be there on the far bank, now that the waters have risen.'"

The Kami replied with a verse: "If you admit that the separation is trying, perhaps you should invite me to live on your side of the Nakagawa." In the evening the rain stopped, and presently he was with us. The conversation fell into the usual pattern. "But you spoke of bending three fingers to count the months," I said, "and now, before you have had time to bend the fourth, another month has gone by."

"About those months of yours," he answered. "When I have suffered my way through the whole series, I will probably be called on to begin again. There is really no sure end to it all. Couldn't we perhaps cut a few pages from the Prince's calendar?"

"We might try calling the wild geese back early," I answered, amused at the suggestion. He laughed heartily. I remembered the Prince and his jealousy, however, and felt compelled to give the conversation a more sober turn. "But in all seriousness I am not as free as you seem to think I am. There is a reason why I cannot take up your suit with the Prince."

"You might let me know what that is at least." And he insisted so strongly that I finally decided to tell him of the Prince's jealousy. I could not bring myself to say the words, however, and, tearing off the sections that I thought it would be best not to let him see, I handed him the Prince's letter. "I suppose I shouldn't be showing this to you," I said, "but I hope it will help you understand the difficulty of my position."

He took the letter and went out to the veranda, where for a long time he appeared to be studying it in the moonlight. It was a dim, misty night.

He gave no indication when he came in of having read the letter. The writing had been quite indistinguishable from the colored background, he said, returning it. He would be back the next day to try again. I replied that I intended to destroy it immediately, but he urged me to wait a bit.

"Time is getting shorter, and people keep telling me that I must watch how I behave myself. It is most depressing," he continued, and for a moment he seemed to be reciting something under his breath. "Well, tomorrow we have a great deal to do at the office. I shall send a messenger around to the boy, and I shall stop by myself."

After he had gone I glanced at the letter beside my pillow, the one I had shown him earlier in the evening, and noticed with surprise that more was missing than I remembered having torn away, apparently including some notes I had made for my poem about the withered autumn grasses.

Early in the morning a letter came from him. He had a bad cold and would not be able to call as he had promised, and could the boy visit him at noon? There seemed no need for haste; the matter was probably as trifling a one as usual, the boy thought. Before he started out, another letter came, more carefully written than the Kami's usual letters: "The reason I wanted so urgently to see you is the matter—I mention it with the greatest reluctance—of that letter. It was indeed a difficult one to read.[150] I realize that I should not ask you to plead my case specially, but if you could now and then mention it in the course of conversation with the Prince—I am filled with gloom at the thought of how ineffectual I seem to be."

There appeared to be nothing there that required an answer. It was hardly necessary to answer every note from him. The next day, however, I began to feel that it would look a bit coy and perhaps cruel of me to ignore him, and I sent off a letter: "Someone here was in penance yesterday, and I did not see your letter until evening. As for my failure to answer immediately, you should take it amiss no more than one resents it when, through no fault of its own, the River Asuka dams up for a time.[151] You suggest that I bring your case up 'in the course of conversation.' Alas, I am in no position to do so. You are not to think, however, that I do not understand your complaints. I suspect that even in broad daylight that letter would be a difficult enough one to read.''

The Kami's house was full of priests when my letter was left at the gate. An answer came early the next morning: ''The house was full of strange people all day, your messenger had gone home, and I was not able to get off a note to you. 'The cuckoo sings its sad song in the shadow of the white flower of lamentation.'[152] What shall I do? May I call to apologize for my remissness?''

''What could have brought forth this?'' I answered. ''My note was meant only to acknowledge your letter of yesterday. 'The cuckoo, far from hiding in the shadow, has been singing its lament quite out in the open.' '' I inked the verse out and wrote instead, in continuation of the first sentences,[153] ''It is all very strange.''

The Commissioner for the Eastern Section of the City[154] died at about that time. The court was in retreat,[155] and many officials were off in mountain temples. I continued to have letters, and now and then a visit, from the Kami.

The Sixth Month came, and the Seventh. With the Eighth Month so close, my extreme concern for the girl, much too young, I thought, to have a suitor, blotted out all my other worries. Then, toward the Twentieth, at a time when the Kami appeared most calm[156] and confident that I would see to bringing the affair to a successful close, I heard that he had run away and was in hiding somewhere with another man's wife, a woman with whom he had had an affair earlier. ''A fine thing for him to have done,'' said my informant. ''Everyone is talking about it.''

I was vastly relieved. I had been wondering, as the appointed time approached, what I could possibly say to forestall him. But what a strange person he was, to behave thus when the goal was in sight.

In due course a letter came from him: ''You have no

doubt heard rumors, shocking ones, about me. But I affirm most strongly that it was not my intention to deceive. And I shall be happy if you remember that I came to you with matters in which you may not tax me with dishonesty.''

"Not your intention to deceive?" I replied. "What can this mean? But in any case I am relieved at this indication that you remember more proper matters.''[157]

In the Eighth Month there was an epidemic of smallpox. It spread to this section of the city toward the end of the month, and my son came down with a severe case. I had practically broken off communication with his father, but the situation was so serious that I felt I really ought to report it to him. I was quite beside myself with worry and uncertainty. Finally I decided that there was no avoiding it and wrote a letter. He sent a very cool reply and once asked through a messenger how the boy was, and that was all. People who need not have done so came to inquire, but he stayed away and thus added a new anguish to my anguish over the boy's illness. Even the Kami, quite unabashedly, came around now and then. From about the first of the Ninth Month, the boy began to recover.

Rains began on about the Twentieth, and continued almost without pause through the better part of the Ninth Month. The Nakagawa here threatened any minute to overflow and join the Kamogawa,[158] taking the house with it. It was a trying time for us. The early rice in front of the house had not yet been gathered, except for small amounts, perhaps what we might use for roasting, that the harvesters had managed to take in during pauses in the rain.

The epidemic continued to grow worse. On the Sixteenth the two sons of the late Minister from the First Ward[159] died. I was saddened and at the same time grateful that my own son had recovered. He was quite well again, but there was no reason yet for him to leave the house.

On about the Twentieth I had a surprising letter from the Prince: "How is the boy? Everyone here has recovered, and why have I not yet see him? I am most worried. You no doubt continue to cherish your resentment, and I for my part, though I have in no sense considered abandoning you, have decided to match your stubbornness. But there are many pleasant memories that will never go.''

I was astonished at the tone of it. I limited my answer, however, to the matter of the boy's health, adding only at the end, ''I must admit to a suspicion that you have indeed forgotten.''

On the first day he left the house, the boy chanced to meet the lady from Yamato[160] going in the opposite direction, and somehow the hubs of their carriage wheels got locked together. The next day he sent her a poem: ''The days and months of my longing become the carriage wheels, and bring upon us incidents such as this.'' Her only reply was a note, heavy with repetition marks,[161] written in at the end of his letter: ''It was not I, not I—you must be mistaken.'' The handwriting was mediocre and the whole tone of the reply made a most unfavorable impression on us.

Late in the Tenth Month, when I was at a relative's house escaping an unlucky omen, I heard that a child had been born to that woman, the one who had been on my mind so much recently.[162] It was an event that would have upset me greatly not very long before, but I took it with complete composure.

Just as we had lighted the lamps that evening, my brother came in with a letter written on Michinoku paper,[163] folded informally, and attached to a plume of dry autumn grass. Who had sent it, I asked as I read it in the lamplight. The handwriting was very much like the Prince's.

''That poem of yours about the withered autumn grass[164] —'Sad indeed the fate of the frost-touched grasses; but would that I were a pony again, to be tamed by those still-fresh grasses'—to what painful thoughts it gives rise.''

It was most odd, his quoting from my letter to the Prince, the one occasioned by that disagreeable letter from him. I asked again who had sent it. The Great Minister in the Horikawa Palace,[165] I suspected. It was indeed he. A messenger had delivered it to the house at Nakagawa and, told that was I was away, had insisted that there was no mistake and that it must be brought to me here. I was at a loss to know how he might have seen my poem, and I asked everyone what I ought to do about the letter. My father was for a reply by return messenger. I do not think myself negligent in these matters, but his insistence seemed a bit obsequious. "'The underbrush in this sad grove is thick, the grass is sere,'" I wrote, "'and the pony that breaks through is in no mood to be tamed.'"

I was told that he started out bravely on an answer but was not able to see it through. The silence that followed my letter was most amusing.

The boy was appointed on very short notice to dance at the interim Hollyhock Festival,[166] and I received one of those rare letters from the Prince. What was to be done, he wondered. With it he sent along all the equipment the boy would need.

On the day of the rehearsal another letter came: "Unfortunately I have suffered a defilement and cannot go to court. I thought I might at least stop by to see him off, but I suppose I would not be welcome. I wonder what I ought to do."

I was filled with consternation at the idea of having to receive the Prince again and hastily sent my son off to his mansion. The Prince was moved to tears,[167] I heard later, and rehearsed a dance with the boy in the garden before sending him to court.

I was determined not to miss the festivities and had my carriage pulled up to wait for the procession. By the curtains that lined the street a palm-frond carriage,[168] not a particularly fine one, was parked with its shades lowered both forward and after. From the sleeves visible beneath the forward shade, several glossy under-robes topped by a layer of lavender, I could see that a woman was inside. A sixth-rank attendant with a long sword came out from the house behind the carriage and, advancing on his knees, said something to whoever was riding in front. My interest attracted, I looked closer. Great numbers of middle and upper-rank officials[169] clustered about the carriage in question, among them several whom I recognized. The procession started by somewhat earlier than usual. Afterwards[170] a knot of high-ranking carriages collected about the lady opposite; they had recognized the Prince's retinue and were reluctant to pass beyond him.

The impression made by the boy and his attendants was creditable indeed, considering the shortness of their preparation. I watched the great men pass out delicacies, listened to their comments, and felt somehow that I had acquired prestige from the events of the day. My father was standing among the lesser officials,[171] not allowed, of course, to approach too near the great carriages. Presently the Prince singled him out and, sending into the house for saké, offered him a cup. This no doubt brought a brief moment of satisfaction.[172]

Someone we knew kept suggesting that my son ought to be married, and there were certain negotiations. Now he was exchanging letters with a lady who seemed to be the daughter of the Governor of Mikawa.[173]

The boy sent this first: "'If we may believe in the sign of the God of Katsuragi,[174] perhaps we may hope for at least a word from you.'"

She did not answer, and he sent again: "'You must have seen those tracks at Yatsuhashi; but in vain I search its many branches for a sign of answering tracks.'"[175]

This time an answer came, but it appeared to have been written by someone else: "'This Yatsuhashi is not for you; you tread its pathways rashly.'"

The boy again: "'Why should the road be difficult—I need only follow the tracks that have gone before.'"[176]

And the lady: "'And where do you propose to find them? The clouds bear no telltale tracks.'"[177]

She seemed determined not to be outdone. The boy again: "'Were there no bridge for the spider, then indeed would our sorrow be great; but as it is...'"[178]

The lady: "'Very well, you have your tracks; and are you to trust to an insecure bridge of clouds?'"[179]

The boy: "'We shall see, we shall see. The crane rarely comes down his cloudy path without a wing to rely on.'"[180]

She sent no reply. It had grown too dark, she said.

The Twelfth Month came, and the boy sent this: "'I have spread a lonely cloak these many years of nights; but never before have I found it wet with morning-after tears.'"

There was no answer, for the lady had gone away somewhere. The next day, when he asked again for an answer, she wrote only, "I saw your letter," and attached it to a branch of brocade tree. He sent back: " " "I saw your letter," and dark, suggestive branches—the affair has taken an unhappy turn.' "[181]

Her answer: " 'The pine on the cloud-capped mountain is an uncertain color.' "[182]

Spring came this year before the old year ended.[183] I sent to tell him of our plans and included a verse: "How I should like, while the old year lasts, to say that to my winter-bound heart too spring has come."

There was no real answer, only a short note: "There is so little time left in the old year, try to get through it without me." And I sent again: " 'If this year too comes fruitlessly to a close, I shall surely be set down as one who never meets the spring.' "

Again there was no answer. I wondered what could be the reason and decided he must have heard he had rivals. That might explain a poem that came from him later: "If it is someone else you await, do not say you wait for me. Let the waves that wash over me be gentle ones."[184]

I answered: " 'Perhaps the waves come, perhaps they do not; but through the years the beach awaits them.' "

Toward the end of the month, I sent this: " 'Cold-hearted waves are these; not the waves but the years pass over the waiting pine.' "

His answer: " 'There are pines that are constant a thousand years; but here the interval between the waves seems short indeed.' "

What, I wondered, could have called forth this outburst. Then, on a very windy day, I sent this: " 'One's thoughts boil up before the wind like the waves of the restless sea.' "[185]

At that he seemed still more annoyed, and a note came back, written by someone else and attached to a branch to which but one leaf was clinging: "The Prince is very busy today."

"How sad," I immediately sent back. " 'There seems no respite from these bare, sad branches. And who has had my affections, I wonder.' "[186]

The weather was fairly good for the rest of the year, with only a few snow flurries. We were busy getting the boy ready for New Year's Day and the Festival of the White Horses.[187] As I oversaw preparation of the gifts he was to take with him, I thought of how quickly the years had gone by, each with the same unsatisfied longing. The old, inexhaustible sadness came back, and I went through the rites for my ancestors[188] but absent-mindedly. Late on the eve of the new year there was a pounding outside. . . .[189]

NOTES TO BOOK ONE

1. Fujiwara Kaneie. He is referred to throughout this translation as "the Prince."

2. Literally "an old-fashioned person." The author's mother or father, probably the former.

3. Several waterfalls seem to have been so designated. This one is probably at Ohara, northeast of Kyoto. The word "shallows" is a conventional reference to a rendezvous.

4. Or "the one who has not seen my letters." The poem is obscure.

5. This poem contains a very common pun: Osaka, the name of a barrier on the road between Kyoto and Lake Biwa, means literally "meeting hill"; hence "to cross Osaka no Seki" signifies in the poetry of the period "to arrange a lovers' meeting."

6. Nakoso no Seki, a barrier in northern Japan between the provinces of Hitachi and Iwaki, not far from the present city of Taira. Nakoso means also "do not come."

7. This coy phrase indicates that the marriage has taken place, and the poems "two mornings later" that the ceremonial rice cakes have been exchanged on schedule. All the poems involved in the courtship are quite conventional, and the four commemorating the wedding are particularly uninteresting. It may be that the author wants to suggest here what a dull marriage it really was from the start.

8. This poem repeats the puns in Kaneie's poem: kure, "log" and "evening," and ōi, "many" and the name of a river.

9. I.e., "I am abandoned and cannot hold back my tears."

10. Perhaps two months after the marriage, the date of which is not clear.

11. Kashiwagi, "oak tree," is a sort of nickname for that branch of the Palace Guards, the Hyōefu, of which Kaneie was at the time an officer. Mori means both "grove" and "guardian," and the same sound is echoed in moru, "to leak through."

12. *Monoimi*. See Introduction, page 18.

13. Ono no Komachi, *Kokinshū* No. 554. "When I am excessively in love, I wear my robe turned inside out in the darkness of the night." A reversed nightgown brings dreams of one's lover.

14. Because of difficulties with forbidden directions, people frequently made token departures and set out in earnest the next morning.

15. There is a reference here to a common metaphor: waves breaking over the pines of this mountain indicate infidelity.

16. On Mt. Hiei, northeast of Kyoto.

17. Several puns, the most important one on *naku*, "to sing" (of a bird) and "to weep." I have translated *uguisu* as "song thrush."

18. This passage is obscure. There is possibly a lacuna.

19. This poem appears in the *Hyakunin Isshu*, the hundred poem cards of the New Year game, and has become easily the most famous in the diary. A pun on *akuru ma*, "the interval before dawn" and also "the interval before the door opens," indicates to Kaneie that she knew he was there and purposely kept him out. This is rather a daring poem.

20. Joshi, the Third Day of the Third Month.

21. Possibly Fujiwara Tamemasa, the author's third cousin and the great-uncle of Murasaki Shikibu, author of the *Genji Monogatari*.

22. A supernatural lady, Hsi Wang Mu, living in the Kun Lun Mountains of China, presented one of the Han emperors with this rare variety of peach. Kaneie's poem may contain a hint that he has had enough of this nagging.

23. This sentence is most unclear. It could refer to more than one wife and it could mean that he regrets ever having taken up company with the author. It could also mean that he is now as indifferent to Michitsuna as to the author herself, and possibly there is a lacuna. "The lady in the main house" is Tokihime, Kaneie's principal wife.

24. *Ne*, "root," means also "sleeping." Hence "where might he be sleeping?"

25. I.e., "he has grown tired of me." The simile of the turning leaves suggests a favorite pun of the author's: *aki*, "autumn," and *aku*, "to weary of."

26. The pun suggested in the author's earlier poem (Note 25) is openly stated here.

27. My translation is only a guess at what this sentence might mean. It seems to contain a reference to a proverb that has been lost. The text reads *taoruru ni tachiyama to tachikaeru*, apparently with a play on the regular recurrence of the syllable *ta*.

28. Possibly a woman, though the text does not say so.

29. Salt was made by burning seaweed.

30. This passage has been interpreted as indicating that the author experienced a sort of hysterical blindness. It can be interpreted quite as well, however, as indicating only extreme absent-mindedness.

31. Not really a bed, but a curtained, slightly raised part of the floor. See Introduction, page 21.

32. *Ya*, "arrow," is also a call used to arouse someone from sleep or inattention. The psychoanalysts have made much of this passage too. The arrow, it seems, has phallic implications.

33. References to spiders in the poetry of this period are vaguely traceable to a very famous poem by Soto-ori-hime, *Kokinshū* No. 1110: "The spider is busy with her web, as though she too were getting ready for a caller this evening." The spider comes generally to stand for a neglectful lover. There has been an ingenious attempt to relate this passage to the *kagerō* of the title. See Introduction, page 8.

34. "How I should like to ask the fish in the traps why he does not come." Written by the daughter of Fujiwara Saneyuki when her lover left her, ostensibly to fetch some fish at Uji, but failed to call even after his return to the city. It appears in both the *Shūishū* (No. 1134) and the *Yamato Monogatari*.

35. *Fumi* means both "book" and "track." *Ato*, "track" or "trace," refers both to bird tracks and to handwriting. Hence the poem refers also to "the place where the book was left."

36. Possibly something to do with the horoscope.

37. Sumai no Sechi, held in the palace in the Seventh Month. This particular year, however, it appears to have been canceled because of the death of one of the Emperor's sisters. *Sumai* in the Heian period was similar to present-day *sumō* except that it was more leisurely and more elaborate, and there was less emphasis on shoving or carrying the opponent out of bounds and more on knocking him off his feet.

38. The next sentence may also be spoken by the mother.

39. Suggesting that Kaneie must have many invitations to choose from, and that the author does not mean to add hers to them.

40. A pun here on *kochi*, "east wind" and "this way." Kaneie's reply would seem to refer to the undependability of the wind in question, since east winds are expected to blow in the spring, not the autumn.

41. The usual pun on *aki*, "autumn," and *aku*, "to weary of."

42. A pun again on *kochi*, "east wind" and "this way."

43. The chronology for this section is unclear. The next event that can be definitely dated in Kaneie's promotion to the fourth rank (page 48), which occurred in 962. Possibly, though there is not much evidence for it, the "long penance"

mentioned on page 47 was occasioned by the death of Kaneie's father, Morosuke. If so, it occurred in 960. Either the other three years are completely missing or they are covered by events which it is not possible to date. My own feeling is that the author, writing considerably later and covering her ground fast, has simply lumped together several years that do not particularly interest her. They would constitute an interlude, a fairly tranquil one to judge from the entries for 962, between the first sad years and the restless years of the pilgrimages described later in Book 1 and in Book 2.

44. The grandson or perhaps great-grandson of an emperor. He is not identified.

45. Or people in general. It is not clear that this refers only to Kaneie. It is also not clear whether he ignored her shortcomings or was not aware of them.

46. *Rei no tokoro*. Tokihime's?

47. The following poems are *chōka,* "long songs," a form not uncommon in the period covered by the *Manyōshū,* but rarer by the time this diary was written. The author's poem consists of 123 *ku,* alternating five- and seven-syllable phrases, and Kaneie's of 89. The two poems are crammed with the standard poetic devices of the period, particularly "pivot words" and puns. Frequently one pun is allowed to suggest another, or an irrelevant phrase is introduced to lead up to a pun. Some of these tricks will be apparent from my translation, and the rest I see no point in giving individual attention to. The author's poem is quite conventional. Kaneie's I think more interesting because it is the only spot in the diary where he is really allowed to give his side of the story.

48. Her father.

49. A river in northern Japan, the sound of whose name suggests "a meeting."

50. A reference to Kaneie's visit after the storm (page 43).

51. I use the personal pronoun for what is often a *double-entendre* making use of natural imagery. Thus the sentence that begins with this line contains several elusive references to falcons and falconing.

52. Michinoku in the author's poem is another name for the province of Mutsu. Obuchi is a village in that province once noted for its horse-breeding. In this and the two following poems the pony is Kaneie, not the author.

53. The rope is Michitsuna (*tsuna,* "rope") and the pony is Kaneie.

54. Shirakawa no Seki was a barrier in the province of Iwashiro in northern Japan. The figure here is of driving horses from the north, where they were bred, to the capital. The *shira* of

Shirakawa suggests the word for "not to know"; hence "I am staying away because I do not know how you will behave." Osaka of course contains the usual pun: "I shall meet you day after tomorrow."

55. Tanabata, the Seventh Day of the Seventh Month, when two stars, the Weaver Maid (Vega) and the Herdsman (Altair) have their annual meeting.

56. As *Shōnagon,* Junior Councilor, the third (fourth if *Sangi,* a sort of supernumerary councilor, is counted) grade of official under the Ministers of the Left, Right, and Center. Only a limited number of fourth-, fifth-, and sixth-grade officials had access to the innermost court.

57. He became *Hyōbu no Tayū,* Vice-Minister of War. The War Ministry apparently was not popular with elegant Heian gentlemen.

58. The Minister of War (*Hyōbukyō no Miya*) appears to have been a son of the Emperor Daigo.

59. The strands of silk of course are love affairs.

60. A *saibara:* "I have taken seven skeins of white thread and woven a cloak for you—leave that woman, come live with me." *Saibara* were folk songs taken up by the Heian nobility.

61. The Minister's poem seems to have homosexual overtones, or perhaps it is to be considered only a conventional flourish. Another possible explanation is that Kaneie's poems are really the author's, and the Minister knows it.

62. Hence a relationship between two men is more secure? This is no better than a guess at what Kaneie's poem might mean. It revolves around the word *yuyushii,* which has two very nearly opposite meanings. If the alternative possibility is taken, then Kaneie might be saying, in answer to the Minister's rather odd poem, that he prefers the company of a lady.

63. It sometimes became necessary to move temporarily to avoid transgressing against a god or to combat an inauspicious omen, a bad dream perhaps. For other examples of this *imitagai* see pages 96, 114. See also Introduction, pages 17-18.

64. *Koiji,* "muddy way" and "way of love" (suggesting unrequited love). Wet sleeves of course indicate tears. Hence, "who among those traveling the way of love does not weep?"

65. Reprimanding Kaneie for his unfaithfulness?

66. Judging from the equanimity with which Kaneie reads the poem, it is probably to be considered a joke.

67. This sentence indicates that Kaneie has promised to call, although there is no such suggestion in Kaneie's letter.

68. In straight *kana.*

69. I.e., he knows perfectly well that Kaneie saw the note, and does not like being put off thus.

70. The semi-annual cleansing of defilements, held at the end of the Sixth Month and the end of the Twelfth Month.

71. The Seventh Day of the Seventh Month. The "penance" (*imi*) here is no doubt the *imitagai* referred to on page 48. It is evidently not as strict as an ordinary *monoimi* since Kaneie feels free to come and go.

72. *Mononoke,* possession by an unfriendly spirit, living or dead. For famous cases of *mononoke,* see "Yugao" and "Aoi" in the *Genji Monogatari.*

73. Assuming that this is the temple "in the western mountains" to which the author goes on her great protest flight in Book 2, then a poem later in the diary indicates that it is at Narutaki. Narutaki lies within the present limits of Kyoto, not far from the Ninnaji (see map: Appendix, Plate 8).

74. *Boni,* the present *O-bon.*

75. The *Kamo* or *Aoi Matsuri,* the festival for the tutelary gods of Kyoto, held the middle of the Fourth Month. The most elaborate of the annual festivals.

76. The rest of the poem, and perhaps more of the text, is missing.

77. An incident not mentioned earlier in the diary, although this sentence suggests that it ought to have been.

78. Possibly the semi-annual purification at the end of the Sixth Month.

79. Or, "how many other omissions I might have made." The sentence is unclear.

80. "Day-closing cicada" might be a more accurate translation. It is heard chiefly in the evening.

81. Kaneie's fourth and least successful son, Michiyoshi, must have been born at about this time, and Kaneie may here be carrying on with the child's mother.

82. The author has been defiled by death and would pass the defilement on to Kaneie if she received him; but he can avoid contamination if he remains standing.

83. Another obscure sentence. It could mean, "But I was still alive, and life was hard."

84. What month is not clear.

85. A village called Miiraku in the Gotō Islands off Nagasaki has been identified as the Mimiraku of this legend. Mimiraku is mentioned in the *Manyōshū* and the *Hizen Fudoki* as a port used in expeditions to the continent. In the following poem, Mimiraku seems to be given a possible literal meaning, "ear pleasure."

86. To avoid defilement.

87. Miharu Arisuke, *Kokinshū* No. 853.

88. Since she is the best equipped member of the family?

89. The last rites for finding a new home for the soul of the deceased.

90. She probably received a token tonsure in preparation for death.

91. Unrin-in, "temple of the cloudy grove." It was at Murasakino, north of the old city but within the limits of the present city of Kyoto.

92. The Priest Sosei, *Kokinshū* No. 947.

93. Possibly the purification took place by a river—hence the image.

94. A sort of zither or psaltery. The principal varieties had six, seven, and thirteen strings.

95. From the description of the leave-taking it would appear that this person is a woman. Whether or not she is the author's sister is not clear.

96. The sister's is a *kouchigi*, an informal outer robe. Presumably the author's is too.

97. *Futaai*, purplish blue with a blue lining.

98. Or saffron: *akakuchiba*.

99. Osaka no Seki, on the road east from Kyoto.

100. *Kuchime*, "decay," is also the name of a famous *wagon,* Japanese *koto*. The same word is taken up by the author in her reply to indicate her tear-drenched sleeves.

101. Part of the text may be missing here.

102. Literally, "at the edge." "Veranda" is possibly not as accurate a translation as it might be.

103. The ailing were kept on "pilgrim's fare," since medical treatment was largely religious.

104. *Goshin,* esoteric Shingon rites.

105. The author sends the first seventeen syllables of the poem, and the ex-rival replies with the concluding fourteen. The author's poem contains puns on *aoi,* "the hollyhock," symbol of the Kamo or Hollyhock Festival, and "meeting day"; and on *tachibana,* "mandarin orange," which suggests "to wait." The poems are interesting chiefly for the picture they give of the author gloating over a defeated rival. It is not possible to say who the rival in question might be.

106. *Tango no Sekku* (or, as here, *Sechi*) the Fifth Day of the Fifth Month. Perhaps livelier than usual this year because the Empress Anshi (Yasuko) died late in the Fourth Month, 964, and thus spoiled the festivities for 964 and 965. The performance the author is so anxious to see is probably the equestrian competition at the palace.

107. *Suguroku,* or *sugoroku*. Each party had fifteen pieces to be moved into enemy territory depending on throws of dice.

108. In various ways iris roots figured in the festivities.

109. I.e., "How can you be sure I will find seats?"

110. Perhaps fifteen or twenty minutes' walk away. That such a distance should be considered formidable gives an interesting suggestion of the closeted life of Heian women.

111. The following poems indicate that the pilgrimage is to the Inari Shrine, southeast of Kyoto. Offerings are still made at various stages on Mt. Inari, and the Kamo Shrines are still divided into the upper and lower branches visited by the author.

112. The pilgrim could tell whether or not his prayers had been heard by seeing whether branches broken from these cedars remained green.

113. The third of the four poems indicates that the pilgrimage is to the Kamo Shrine northeast of Kyoto, tutelary shrine for the city.

114. A traditional shrine decoration, whose mention here adds little to the meaning of the poem. The sacred tree is the *sakaki,* a broad-leaf evergreen; strands of bark cloth (*yuu*) were suspended from its branches.

115. Worn when making offerings, and introduced here to present the idea of the author's suffering ("bound") heart.

116. *Ise Monogatari:* "Harder than piling eggs ten times ten, to love one who does not love in return."

117. The Palace of the Ninth Ward was the residence of Kaneie's father, Morosuke. Only one of Kaneie's sisters, Fushi (Yoshiko), seems to answer the description here, and she did not become consort to the Emperor Reizei until the following year. Such errors in dating, and there are a number, confirm the theory that much of the diary was written considerably after the incidents recorded. "Imperial Concubine" might be a more accurate translation for the lady's position.

118. Prince Morihira, later the Emperor En-yū.

119. Reizei, second son of Murakami, the deceased Emperor. Kaneie's nephew.

120. *Tōgū no Suke,* the third-ranking official in the Crown Prince's household.

121. *Kurōdo no Tō,* one of the two heads of the *Kurōdodokoro,* Imperial Secretariat, a key organization which had by this time taken over many of the prerogatives of the Council of State.

122. Kaneie's sister Tōshi (Tomiko), a rather notorious lady who appears several more times in the diary. She captured the affections of the Emperor Murakami while her husband (the Emperor's brother) and the Empress (her sister Anshi or Yasuko) were still living, and after both of them had died she moved into the palace and monopolized the Emperor's attention.

123. Shide no Yama, a mountain in the Land of the Dead.

124. To find a new home for the soul of the deceased.

125. *Hyōe no Suke,* the second-ranking officer in one of six divisions of the Palace Guards. Fujiwara Sukemasa, Kaneie's second cousin.

126. *Amagumo,* "rain clouds," suggests also "nun's clouds."

127. Kaneie became the former in 967, the latter in 968.

128. This is most unclear. Perhaps the text is garbled.

129. Callers on Kaneie?

130. The Priest Sosei, *Shūishū* No. 5: "It is the song of the thrush we await this New Year's morn."

131. Puns here on *koi,* "love" and "a swollen leg"; and *ōgo,* "a carrying pole" and "a meeting time"; hence, "for all the sorrows of our one-sided love, we have yet our lovers' meetings." The significance of putting legs on chestnuts is not clear. The text may be mutilated.

132. Jōganden repeats the author's puns and adds a suggestion that she is less fortunate in the matter of lovers' meetings than the author: *miru,* "to see" and also a kind of seaweed, seems to indicate that the author at least has someone to look after her.

133. This apparently refers to the eating of a porridge called *mochigayu* on the Fifteenth of the First Month.

134. There is an oblique reference here to a poem from the *Ise Monogatari:* "Do not undo your under-apron for another, although the morning-glory waits not for the evening." If, as the commentators suggest, the gentleman is Jōganden's lover, then his letter comes to seem rather insulting. Possibly it is Kaneie and he is being funny: he would like to call on his sister Jōganden, but he fears the author's jealousy.

135. A very famous "eastern song" (*azuma uta*), *Kokinshū* No. 1093: "If ever I am unfaithful to you, that day the waves will break over Sue no Matsuyama." Hence the figure of waves breaking over a pine mountain (*matsuyama*) stands for a lover's fickleness. The author seems here to suggest that the gentleman might be fickle, but surely not with someone as chaste as Jōganden. There is perhaps a touch of irony in the exchange.

136. If the sender of the original letter ("I feel that I really must call on you . . .") is Kaneie, then this poem would mean, with a very common pun on *matsu,* "pine tree" and "to wait," that it is the thought of the author, who waits patiently, which excites Kaneie.

137. The text says merely "over there." Since Kaneie is near-by, and since he is Jōganden's brother, it is not unlikely that his mansion is the one referred to.

138. Autumn began with the Seventh Month, in spite of the hot weather.

139. The exchange of poems is in general a debate over which of the two ladies is the more forlorn.

140. A temple south of Nara. It is called "Hatsuse" here. The text is translated as literally as possible, but the repetition of the words *omoitatsu* and *tatamu tsuki* in the short space of two sentences suggests a garble.

141. Or *Daijōsai*, the first harvest festival after the accession of a new Emperor. The festival proper was held in the Eleventh Month, the preliminary purification in the Tenth.

142. *Nyōgodai.* Kaneie's daughter (and Tokihime's) Chōshi (Yukiko).

143. A temple just beyond the southeast corner of the old city of Kyoto, not far from the present Tōfukuji. It is no longer standing.

144. Uji, eight or nine miles southeast of Kyoto, was the site of celebrated villa, the Uji no In, built in the ninth century by Minamoto Tōru. The author's itinerary, though some of the places mentioned cannot be identified, follows roughly the present road south from Kyoto to the vicinity of the town of Miwa, from where it turns east to the Hasedera (see map: Appendix, Plate 8).

145. *Ajiro,* screens of woven wood or bamboo set upright in the river.

146. The road from Tsubaichi (the present town of Miwa) to the Hasedera is short; the author must therefore have started out late. The scenery is rather gentler than her description suggests.

147. Or perhaps her clothing seems faded and tired in comparison with the radiance outside.

148. *Mo,* a woman's formal outer garment, tied at the waist and trailing behind (see illustration: Appendix, Plate 4). Here it appears that the author has been dressed informally and is putting on a *mo* in preparation for arriving at the temple; or perhaps she stretches one over the back of the carriage, to admire the effect.

149. It is not clear whether *kuchiba,* "withered leaves," in this sentence refers to the real thing or to a color. If the latter, then the translation would better be, "Dust had settled on my lavender (*usuiro*) train, which modulated well into the russet of the skirt underneath."

150. Whether from insomnia or the requirements of the pilgrimage is not clear.

151. Although the trip to the temple took four days, not counting the night spent at the Hōshōji.

152. Near Uji.

153. *Zuijin,* men of the *Kon-efu* assigned to guard certain officials. Why the guard should have "overtaken" the author's party is not explained. He would be expected to approach from Uji, toward which they are headed.

154. It is not clear who sends the first poem. If it is Kaneie, and the reply the author's, the meanings become a good deal different. The first would indicate that he might as well ask the fish at Uji as try to get a statement from her on when she will be back, and the second would be her counterthrust, an inquiry as to precisely what new interest has lured him so far from home.

155. *Zō,* a third-level official, but of what part of the bureaucracy is not specified.

156. *Efu no Suke,* leaving it unclear to which branch of the Guards the gentleman belongs. Possibly Michitaka, Kaneie's oldest son.

157. *Kariginu,* an informal outer robe worn by men for outdoor pursuits (see illustration: Appendix, Plate 5).

158. A vegetarian diet.

159. *Azechi no Dainagon,* originally an official sent from the capital to inspect local governments, after the Chinese fashion, but by this time a sinecure. The person referred to here is Kaneie's uncle, Morouji.

160. *Hitoeginu,* an unlined under-robe.

161. Both of these remarks seem to have been very witty, but the point is largely lost on the modern reader. The conjunction of sun and moon and of flowers and fruit is congratulatory.

162. They had only two wheels; hence the shafts had to be propped up.

163. See Note 141, above.

164. *Daijōe no kemi,* literally "the inspection of the grain for the *Daijōe.*" It is not known exactly what this term refers to. It may be the *Daijōe* itself, since that ceremony was basically an inspection of the first samples of the harvest.

NOTES TO BOOK TWO

1. It is not possible to keep the author's relatives distinct one from another. Whether this is the sister who left for the provinces on page 55, or the sister who left the author's house on page 39, or neither, or both, is not clear. In fact it is not even clear whether it is a sister or a brother.

2. Literally, "sew heaven and earth into a bag." Court ladies recited a verse about such bags on New Year's Day to bring the fulfillment of their wishes.

3. *Tenke no ehō. Tenke* was "the temper of the skies," *ehō* was the lucky direction for the year. The two seem to be lumped together here to indicate good charms and portents in general.

4. An intercalary month was introduced every thirty months to keep the seasons from going askew under the lunar calendar.

5. Literally, "between the men here and the men there." This passage has generally been taken to refer to a quarrel between the author's retinue and that of either Kaneie or Tokihime. Recently, however, there has been a theory that the quarrel was rather between Kaneie's men and those of his uncle and political rival, Morotada, and that the author's men were also involved.

6. We learn later that the author's house was under repair, possibly damaged in the riot. The notion of returning to one's native village triumphantly clad in brocade is Chinese.

7. The Third Day of the Third Month.

8. The lady mentioned in Note 22, Book 1, who presented the Emperor Han Wu with the three-thousand-year peach. Here her name seems to signify a peach connoisseur, and by extension a good toper. Possibly the poem is written by the author. That would explain its being included in the diary.

9. Religious offerings were, and still are, taken down and consumed.

10. The two parties being the Fore and the After.

11. A rather feminine metaphor, but here there seems no alternative to applying it to the archers themselves. Literally, it is "willow cocoons" which open, with a pun on "relaxed eyebrows," to indicate comfort and confidence.

12. Minamoto Takaaki, son of the Emperor Daigo. He was exiled ostensibly for plotting an insurrection in favor of his son-in-law, Prince Tamehira, a disappointed candidate for Crown Prince after the accession of the Emperor Reizei. See Introduction, page 15.

13. Atago is northwest of the city, Kiyomizu southeast of the old city and within the present city. The text says "Kiyoshiho," which could be the result of a misreading and miscopying of "Kiyomizu," or of "Kiyotaki," to which the author herself flees later in Book 2.

14. *Sochi* (a variant of *Sotsu*), the Kyushu Viceroy. Takaaki was actually made *Gon no Sotsu*, "Provisional" or "Honorary" Viceroy, a favorite title for banished statesmen.

15. This was a thirteen-month year. See Note 4 above.

16. *Keshiyaki*, "burning of poppy seeds," a Shingon rite.

17. Evidently a new mansion.

18. I.e., "If I go to heaven and not to hell, I shall be watching you."

19. *Karabitsu,* a lacquer box or chest set on short legs.
20. The *Tsukinami no Matsuri,* at which offerings were distributed to imperially favored Shinto shrines, and the semiannual purgation of defilements. Both were held in the Sixth and Twelfth Months.
21. The wife of Minamoto Takaaki, who was exiled (pages 72-73). She was Kaneie's sister.
22. North of the palace.
23. Another *chōka.* See Note 47, Book 1.
24. The Fourth Month was the "Month of the *Unohana.*" *Unohana* is a white-flowering shrub, *deutzia scabra,* the dictionaries say. The first syllable does double duty, suggesting also "sorrow" or "gloom."
25. There was an intercalary Fifth Month in 969. The Fifth Month of the lunar calendar is in theory the rainy season (*samidare,* "Fifth-Month rain").
26. "The ninefold court" is a standard epithet, perhaps imported from China. The "nine counties and two islands" refers to Kyushu (nine provinces plus the islands of Iki and Tsushima).
27. A *chōka* by Ise, *Kokinshū* No. 1006, contains this sentence: "Where am I to turn in my loneliness? I am like the fisherman at Ise whose boat has gone adrift."
28. The Sixth Month.
29. Oaraki, in the province of Yamato, suggests great sorrows.
30. Fujiwara Takamitsu, brother of Kaneie and of Takaaki's wife, left Kyoto to become a priest early in 962, first on Mt. Hiei and later on Tōnomine, a mountain south of Nara. He is the principal subject (the compilation seems to have been by someone else) of a journal, largely poetic, called the *Takamitsu Nikki* or *Tōnomine Shōshō Monogatari.* The author here plans the details of her letter to substantiate the story that it comes from the hermit at Tōnomine: it is on gray *kanyagami,* official paper (perhaps lending a certain austerity), folded formally (*tatebumi*) instead of being twisted or knotted like an ordinary social or romantic note, and attached to a split or frayed stick the precise nature of which is unclear but which possibly has religious connotations.
31. In the Yoshino district south of Nara.
32. Because Kaneie has moved? The house to which she now returns is presumably the one that was too close to him on page 71, and the one from which she moved on page 63.
33. Tokihime's? Jōganden's?
34. I.e., *tatebumi* as before.
35. She had someone else write it? Why a child is not explained.
36. The saltmaker's fire suggests dripping salt water (salt was

made by burning seaweed); hence, tears; hence, "Will you not notice my tears?" The wind seems to stand for the author's letter.

37. Fujiwara Morotada, Kaneie's uncle. Actually the celebration seems to have taken place in the Seventh Month, not the Eighth as the author has it.

38. *Saemon no Kami*. It has not been established who he was. Fujiwara Morouji (Kaneie's uncle), Fujiwara Naritoki (Kaneie's cousin), and Minamoto Masanobu (later Michitsuna's father-in-law) have all been suggested.

39. Possibly because of the incident described on page 71 (see Note 5 above).

40. The name of the sand plover, *chidori*, literally "thousand bird," is, according to one theory, in imitation of its cry.

41. East of Kyoto. The last pass before the Tōkaidō enters the city.

42. Traditionally the best moon of the year.

43. Indicating that it was a small house. Large mansions were surrounded by earthen walls.

44. All of these poems are vaguely suggestive of long life and prosperity. In this one the full moon carries that suggestion. There is a pun on *kochiku*, "come this way" and a kind of bamboo flute.

45. Pines and cranes are symbolic of long life. The poem about the pines may be interpreted as meaning that our hearts all turn to this glad occasion.

46. Ladies' carriages were to be distinguished by sleeves trailing tastefully from under the curtains (see illustration: Appendix, Plate 5).

47. This poem and the one about the fish traps suggest the passage of time; hence, a long life.

48. Among the events of little consequence was the abdication of the Emperor Reizei.

49. The two sides again being the Fore and the After.

50. The O were a line of court music and dance masters.

51. *Kochōraku*, a child's dance in imitation of butterflies. Here it is apparently danced by an adult.

52. *Hitoe*, an unlined under-robe.

53. *Tenjō-bito*, officers of the fourth, fifth, and sixth ranks who were admitted to the Inner Court.

54. This passage contains a number of terms that appear to be technical, and it is not easy to see exactly what is happening. Possibly the author herself does not have a very clear idea.

55. Possibly Tamemasa's son Nakakiyo. Since a "captain of the Guards" would be a little old for this sport, it has been suggested that perhaps the son of some such person is meant. It

has also been suggested that the text is garbled, and that two boys, not one, are meant.

56. *Ryōō*, a dance about a Chinese general who was so handsome that he had to wear a mask in battle to keep from distracting his soldiers. It was a *sabu*, a "left" or "Chinese" dance, as distinguished from a "right" or "Korean" dance. Michitsuna's seems to have been a "Korean" dance.

57. The incident is recorded in the *Nihon Giryaku*. The robe was a scarlet one.

58. *Kandachime*, third rank and above (fourth and above in the case of *Sangi* councilors).

59. A possible interpretation is that Kaneie was confined to his home for seven or eight days, but it does not seem likely that he would use a grand word like *ōtono*, "great mansion," in describing his own place. The "Minister," however, is only a convenience for translation.

60. Fujiwara Saneyori, Kaneie's uncle, the Regent (*Sesshō*) and Great Minister of State (*Dajōdaijin*). Kaneie's brother Koretada succeeded to the Regency.

61. The Sixth Month.

62. On Lake Biwa, in the province of Omi.

63. The semi-annual purgation of defilements, here the end of the Sixth Month.

64. Michitsuna seems to have gone along, but whether there were three besides or three including him is not clear. The author's route follows approximately the present road to Otsu, from where it turns north along the lake shore (see map: Appendix, Plate 8).

65. Abandoned by her husband? The text is extremely vague.

66. Osaka no Seki.

67. *Ochi*. "Pride of India," according to the dictionaries.

68. The following section is perhaps the murkiest in the diary, obscurity piled on obscurity. Certain difficulties are explained away (that of cutting among the small boats, for instance) if it is assumed that the last stage of the journey is by boat, but then new difficulties appear. I have not come upon a completely satisfactory interpretation. This may perhaps be put down as a not very competent bit of narrative.

69. The text seems to suggest either a change of direction or a change of conveyances, though there would seem to be no good reason for either.

70. Whose? This section suggests more of a retinue than we are told the author has. Perhaps other parties have arrived for the purification.

71. This is only a guess. The proverb, if such there be, has not been identified.

72. These seem to be ladies, but what ladies we are not told. The author did not bring along any lady attendants, and is accompanied only by the lady "in the same situation" as she, and maybe one other.

73. Possibly some gay ladies in another party are displaying themselves wantonly.

74. It is not likely that the offerings for a purification would be so exciting. Images in the nature of scapegoats have perhaps been floated out onto the lake.

75. "Sasanami," a rather earthy *kagura*, which introduces its own set of obscurities. To take one possible interpretation: "Challenge: 'That's a pretty girl there, pounding rice at Karasaki in Shiga. Say, pretty girl, can't we get you to take one of us for a husband?' Response: 'You make about as much sense as a crab waving its claws in the air. It must be because you haven't been able to find a girl who will marry you.' "

76. *Higurashi,* the "day-long cicada" of page 51; heard principally in the evening in late summer and autumn. Also called the *kana-kana* cicada in imitation of its hum.

77. The poem game of page 59 again. There are puns here on Hashirii, literally "running well," and Shimizu, "clear water." This Shimizu, in the vicinity of Osaka no Seki, does not seem to be the Shimizu at which the author stopped for lunch on the way to Karasaki. The latter would be north of Otsu, but exactly where is not known.

78. Lightning was believed to make rice head. *Inabikari,* "lightning," is literally "rice light."

79. Fujiwara Tōshi, Kaneie's sister.

80. *Naishi no Kami,* one of two principal officers in the women's quarters of the palace. The position rose in prestige from the ninth century, and Tōshi's status was about equivalent to that of an imperial concubine. She actually became *Naishi no Kami* in 969, not 968.

81. Possibly the rivalry between Kanemichi and Kaneie. Kaneie, the younger of the two, was rising faster in the world than Kanemichi thought appropriate. Tōshi may have been nearer Kanemichi; her daughter became his wife.

82. Occasionally, as in this sentence, the author uses verb endings usually reserved for the actions of another in a sense that can only describe her own. She seems to switch uncertainly from what we might call first-person to third-person narrative and back again.

83. The hawk is Michitsuna, and there is a pun on *soru,* "to fly off" and "to take the tonsure."

84. *Boni, O-bon.*

85. Ki no Tsurayuki, *Gosenshū* No. 1190: "I am a sad figure,

wanting to renounce the world but knowing of no way to do it.''

86. Fujiwara Saneyori. The lady is possibly the daughter of Kuniaki and the mother of Kaneie's daughter Suishi (Yasuko). The daughter of Kuniaki is mentioned in the *Eiga Monogatari* as the *tai no kata*, a designation which would indicate that she was more successful than the author and was taken into Kaneie's main mansion. Like the author, she belonged to a minor branch of the Fujiwara clan.

87. A romance between Kaneie and the third daughter of the Emperor Murakami is recorded in the *Eiga Monogatari*. When it began is not known.

88. The Ishiyama-dera (temple), south of Otsu in the province of Omi.

89. As we discover later, she has some twenty attendants. We may perhaps assume that she starts out with a few and is overtaken by a few more.

90. The author's route again follows generally the present road to Otsu. From Uchidenohama in the present city of Otsu she takes a boat to the Ishiyama-dera. She seems to make the trip to Otsu on foot.

91. This functionary has not been identified.

92. This sentence piles three adjectives one on another, a most unusual device and a most intense expression of melancholy.

93. This clause seems to be garbled.

94. *Katakishi,* a strange word in this context, seems to indicate that only side of the valley is wooded.

95. *Goya,* "post-midnight."

96. Possibly *dokudami,* a rather smelly weed whose leaves and root were used as medicine. The commentators disagree.

97. Or "citron," *yu.*

98. This incident is recorded in the "Ishiyama-dera Engi Emaki,'' a picture scroll dating from the late Kamakura or early Muromachi period and preserved in the Ishiyama-dera (see illustration: Appendix, Plate 7). The caption on the scroll, no doubt for propaganda purposes, says that because of this benevolent sign from the Buddha the author and Kaneie were reconciled.

99. The original is less clear. Something about the boat surprises.

100. A popular song of the day?

101. Near the point where the Seta River flows from Lake Biwa. There are other literary references to Yamabukinosaki and Ikagasaki, but neither place has been identified.

102. In the Seventh Month.

103. *Tokoro,* which usually stands for *Kurōdodokoro.* See Note 121, Book 1.

104. Subjects and objects are not very clearly distinguished in this passage.

105. *Utaishō,* head of one branch of the Palace Guards.

106. The first Harvest Festival after the accession of a new Emperor (Reizei abdicated in 969, and En-yū succeeded to the throne). Michitsuna does not seem to have actually received his rank until after the *Daijōe.*

107. Since Michitsuna did not receive his first official position until 974, this would involve chiefly the assigning of estates and a consequent income. Kaneie's friendliness with the ex-Emperor Reizei has been noted earlier in the diary (see page 62).

108. Probably Minamoto Kaneaki, a son of the Emperor Daigo.

109. The theory perhaps being that since the forbidden period was almost over, this could constitute but a slight transgression.

110. The following section again is obscure.

111. It is not clear who says this, or to whom it refers. It could be either sympathy for the author or admiration for Kaneie.

112. This sentence contains some odd words, and is not at all clear. It could possibly mean that Kaneie helped less than he should, and the author herself was as a result frantically busy.

113. Possibly for the investiture after the *Daijōe.* If, however, this and the courtesy calls in the next paragraph have to do with the investiture, it has most likely already taken place, and records which put it in the Twelfth Month are inaccurate.

114. The text does not indicate who is living in the "south apartment," nor is it clear exactly where that would be. The south would be the front of the house, an unlikely spot for a lady's quarters.

115. The daughter of Kuniaki?

116. *Kokinshū* No. 28, author unknown.

117. The weeks of the spring and autumn equinoxes, here the spring equinox. The occasion for a week-long Buddhist festival, possibly Shinto in origin.

118. *Uwamushiro* being changed for *tadanomushiro* in preparation for the austerity of the retreat.

119. Which is to say: "Now even the marriage bed is going."

120. Apparently a belief of the time. I have not found an explanation for it.

121. The text says only that "there was to be a child." The sister is an invention.

122. She seems in fact not to have gone until the Sixth Month.

123. Gyōgi Bosatsu was a famous and ubiquitous priest of the Nara period. This incident is recorded in the *Fusō Ryakki.*

124. Cf. Note 18 above.

125. Fujiwara Asatada, *Gosenshū* No. 70: "Now, when the flowers are in bloom, I want only to leave the world for a deserted mountain."

126. In addition to the hazard of forbidden directions, there were occasions on which the place where one was living became untenable if one was to avoid tramping on a god. This appears to be such an occasion. See Introduction, pages 17-18.

127. Another obscure clause.

128. Part of the text is missing here. The author is apparently still at her father's when it picks up again.

129. Irises were (and still are) laid on the roof on the *Tango no Sekku,* the Fifth of the Fifth Month.

130. Because it would be barred for the *monoimi. Monoimi* was in some respects a stricter regimen than the *nagashōji* (a Buddhist pilgrimage or retreat) which the author has been undergoing. Both here and in the *imitagai* described in Book 1 (pages 48–50) Kaneie seems to feel free to come and go. The use of "penance" to designate this last occurrence may be objected to as not adequately distinguishing it from *monoimi,* but the point does not seem worth fretting over.

131. *Shita matsu,* "waiting under," also suggests "secretly hoping." The author's poem indicates folding the marriage quilt —leaving him for good. Hence the haste with which he comes to see her in spite of his penance.

132. Cf. *Fujiwara Nakabumi Shū:* "I may go to the mountains, but unless I quite renounce the world I shall have no callers."

133. The incident described on page 50?

134. Possibly a reference to a proverb. The meaning is not as clear as the translation seems to make it.

135. *Sasashite,* "doing such and such," possibly indicating that Kaneie is on his way in spite of the *monoimi.*

136. There is some confusion in the use of, or the failure to use, honorifics in this letter. It perhaps arises from the author's failure to make a clear distinction between direct and indirect discourse.

137. Or possibly she is charging Michitsuna with having unnecessarily excited Kaneie.

138. Menstruation.

139. *Soya,* in contrast to the "pre-dawn rites," page 89.

140. One *chō,* about 120 yards.

141. The call of the thrush: *hitoku, hitoku,* "someone's coming, someone's coming."

142. Ise, *Gosenshū* No. 172: "The cuckoo singing before the dawn, and I am awake at the first call and waiting for the second." Whether the author's annoyance was at being roused by the cuckoo or at not hearing it again is not clear.

143. Or "grouse," *kuina*.
144. In a Shinto shrine. An illustration of the merger of Shinto and Buddhism.
145. *Takayaka*, meaning here uncertain.
146. Literally, "and another came back." The aunt who had returned to the city?
147. A wild guess. The text seems to be mutilated.
148. *Rui shitaru hito*. It is by no means clear that this refers to the aunt.
149. Possibly someone from Kaneie's household. Michitaka, Kaneie's eldest son, has been suggested, but the suggestion does not seem a very good one. The gentleman talks like someone older than the author.
150. *Agame tatematsure*, an extreme and here sarcastic honorific.
151. Literally, "the people in the western section of the city." This is generally taken to refer to the author's household. At only one place in the first two books of the diary (page 60) are we told where she is living, and that is in the eastern section of the city. It has also been suggested that this refers to the wife of the exiled Takaaki. (See Note 12 above.)
152. This paragraph is unclear.
153. *Imoyu*, or *imori*, a Buddhist fast day.
154. *Kokinshū* No. 888, author unknown: "Among the proud and the low-born alike are those who have known better days." Hence, "Mean as I am, I am able to understand what has happened to her."
155. *Odamaki*, an oblique literary reference to the lower classes, indicating that the writer has caught the poetic allusion.
156. This seems to be a place name, but it has not been identified.
157. Narutaki is in the western outskirts of the present city of Kyoto. See map: Appendix, Plate 8.
158. *Sumu mizu*, "clear waters," also suggests "waters that do not go back."
159. Fujiwara Tōshi (Tomiko), Kaneie's sister.
160. South of the old city, but within the present city.
161. *Otoshitarikeri*, literally "he dropped it." How the poem reaches the author is not clear, since it would involve a conspicuous detour for the gentleman to deliver it, or even "drop it," himself.
162. A mountainous district in the Kii Peninsula.
163. I am not sure whether he is upbraiding the author or sympathizing with her. Both interpretations seem possible.
164. *Hyōe no Suke*, second in command of one section of the Palace Guards. This time it does seem to be Michitaka, Kaneie's eldest son.
165. Ritual purification.

166. As a child he would have been permitted to see the author; now, as a young man, he would not be (she receives him from behind a curtain).

167. Michitsuna.

168. *Kokinshū* No. 509, author unknown: "My heart is as unsettled as the bobs the fishermen use at Ise."

169. *Nadeshiko wa nade ōshitari ya.* The cleverness of the remark comes in part from the repetition of *nade.*

170. Because he has violated the tabooed direction tonight. One reading of the text has it as a six-day penance.

171. The author is still on pilgrim's fare, a vegetarian diet.

172. Another difficult sentence, and another indication of the author's apparent inability to express her feelings clearly.

173. Fujiwara Tōshi? The *Gyokuyōshū* attributes this poem to Fujiwara Kanshi. Tōshi appears first in Book 1 of this diary as *Jōganden no ōnkata* and, after several reappearances, emerges in Book 2 as *Naishi no Kami,* the designation used here. Kanshi, on the other hand, has not appeared before. It therefore seems likely that the *Gyokuyōshū,* which was compiled late in the Kamakura period, or some three and a half centuries after this diary was written, is mistaken and that the poem is Tōshi's.

174. The Yoshino River flows between two mountains, Imo, "Wife," and Se, "Husband," and comes therefore to stand for wedlock.

175. Ono Bizai, *Kokinshū* No. 560: "My love is like the mountain grasses: no matter how deep it grows, no one knows of it."

176. A reference to the fact that the Yoshino in its lower reaches changes its name to the Kino.

177. It is Tanabata, when the celestial lovers have their unusual meeting.

178. Evidently another example of a fixed spot become untenable. See Introduction, pages 17-18.

179. Where they have gone for purification. It is not identified.

180. Fujiwara Morouji. See page 68.

181. *Ajiro byōbu,* woven of narrow strips of bamboo, bark, or reeds.

182. *Kichō,* movable curtains suspended from wooden frames.

183. *Kuchi mumage ni,* an expression which does not appear in the other principal works of the period. Possibly a vulgarism.

184. The Kasuga Shrine, tutelary shrine of the Fujiwara clan, is at the foot of Mikasa-yama ("Mountain of the Three Umbrellas" or, more accurately, "Mountain of the Three Rain Hats") in the present city of Nara. It can have been only a slight detour for the author and her party, in spite of her description of the arduous journey.

185. A *saibara*: "By the Well of Asuka, by the Well of Asuka, it is good to stay; the shade is inviting, the water is cool, the grass is sweet." The well of this song was at the Asuka Shrine, a considerable distance south of Nara and not on the route the author seems to have taken. The temple where she pauses is probably the Gankōji, also known as the Asuka-dera, in Nara.

186. Or received them. It is not clear who does the bestowing.

187. See map: Appendix, Plate 8.

188. The text for this and the next two sentences seems to be mutilated.

189. On the occasion of the *sumō* tournament; annually in the Seven Month.

190. Unclear. Possibly there is a reference to a proverb or poem.

191. A reference perhaps to the dream (page 90) which was taken as a sign that the Buddha had noticed her.

192. It is possible that this sentence is a part of one of the two letters, but not easy to say why there should be such an outburst from Kaneie.

193. The god Isonokami thrives on rain. See Note 116, Book 3.

194. *Tsumado,* a hinged door in the corner of the room.

195. Unspecified.

196. There was a belief that a dead frog could be revived by covering it with a plantain (*ōbako*) leaf.

197. A pun on *amagaeru,* "rain frog" and "nun returns."

198. Perhaps the lady known as Omi (the daughter of Kuniaki?).

199. The gods of pestilence were exorcised on the last day of the year.

NOTES TO BOOK THREE

1. This is the only mention in the diary of a specific date. It has been taken as evidence that the author is treating of recent events.

2. The Emperor bowed to the four directions early on New Year's morning to insure prosperity for the coming year. Possibly a similar ritual was observed in aristocratic houses.

3. Written "white horse," but pronounced "green horse." A ceremony on the Seventh of the First Month, at which the Emperor inspected twenty-one horses in the palace grounds. By the time of this diary they seem to have become white horses, but originally they were dark horses with a greenish tinge, symbolic of the reviving vigor of spring.

4. A pun on Futara, the old name of the present Nikkō, which also suggests "lid."

5. *Tsukasameshi,* the annual appointments (not including ministers) for the capital.

6. *Dainagon,* the first level under minister on the Council of State.

7. *Uchigi.*

8. *Nōshi,* the ordinary dress for lounging about the house. See illustration: Appendix, Plate 4. The text is obscure here, and it is not entirely clear whether the robe is starched or wrinkled.

9. Straw matting covered with oiled silk.

10. I.e., he cut across one of the two forward corridors. See Introduction, page 20.

11. The text says literally "and it is falling now." She may be writing of the present, or the "now" may indicate, as in the translation, that snow continues to fall even after reaching this remarkable depth.

12. *Sōnokoto,* a thirteen-stringed *koto.*

13. A four-stringed mandolin-like instrument.

14. Her own house, or her father's? We are not told when she went home.

15. The Kasuga Shrine at Nara was the seat of the Fujiwara tutelary god. Messengers were sent from court with offerings for its semi-annual festivals.

16. *Darani,* esoteric Shingon incantations.

17. In addition to doing without animal foods, this priest does without cereals.

18. Only officers of ministerial rank were permitted such gates. Actually they seem to have had six pillars, two central and four flanking.

19. *Daijin Kugyō,* a term covering all officials of the third rank and above and all Councilors (*Sangi*) of the fourth rank and above.

20. Several phrases in this section indicate that the author is writing of the very recent past.

21. The Regency has by this time passed into Kaneie's immediate family. See Introduction, page 15.

22. *Saishō,* another name for *Sangi,* a sort of supernumerary Councilor ranking just under *Dainagon* and *Chūnagon* on the Council of State. Kanetada seems to have been a grandson of the Emperor Yōzei, although there is some inconsistency in the genealogical tables. This is one of the rare appearances in the diary of a personal name.

23. On the west shore of Lake Biwa, south of Mt. Hiei.

24. This could mean, with the usual play on Osaka no Seki, that Kaneie has succeeded in forming a liaison; it seems here to indicate, however, that the lady was actually living beyond the barrier in the province of Omi when Kaneie visited her.

25. It is not clear why they laugh. It may be at the repetition of

the travel image in the lady's poem, but if so it is hard to see why her poem is any more gauche than Kaneie's; or perhaps the way in which she throws Kaneie's imagery back at him is considered not very imaginative.

26. The text seems to be mutilated here.

27. Or perhaps, though it does not seem very likely, she writes of her difficulties with Kaneie. The text is vague.

28. *Ajiroguruma,* an oxcart with sides of woven bark, reeds, or bamboo. A courtier of Michitsuna's modest rank would normally ride in one, a more exalted official only on very informal occasions.

29. Literally, "the place I so disliked." The daughter of Kuniaki again?

30. This seems to indicate that Kaneie's mansion is south of the author's, and that, in order to be able to proceed in a propitious direction on his return there, it is necessary now, the evening before, to move to a more appropriate jumping-off spot.

31. Possibly Tokihime's daughter Senshi (Akiko), later consort of the Emperor En-yū and mother of the Emperor Ichijō. She would be a little younger than the author's adopted daughter.

32. Reizei.

33. Because he had come unadorned the night before?

34. Possibly the pilgrimage on page 61.

35. The text for this and the preceding sentence is badly mutilated.

36. Kitano is north and west of, and Funaoka north of, the old palace, while the Kamo Shrine is northeast of the old palace. This is an odd route for the author to follow unless living in the western section of the city. (See Note 151, Book 2.)

37. *Manyōshū* No. 1839: "It is for you that I wet my skirts in the melting snow, gathering the swamp grasses of Yamada." The poem seems to have no particular pertinence to the present situation.

38. The intercalary Second Month has thrown the seasons late this year.

39. At the Iwashimizu Hachiman Shrine, southwest of Kyoto, sacred to the war god, Hachiman, and his mother, the Empress Jingū. This would be the interim festival (*rinjisai*), held in the Third Month.

40. It is not easy to see what is happening here. The author and her "relative" would probably not be going to the shrine, rather a formidable distance, and if they were going they could hardly be back before dark; and it is still early for them

to be going out to watch the procession. But they go some-where.

41. *Birō* (short for *birōgeguruma*), a carriage with sides of woven palm fronds.

42. The seat of the retired Emperor, not far from the present Nijō Castle.

43. Or possibly it is the author who is pleased that there is not a large crowd. The great frequency of the character for "per-son" in this passage has led to a theory that there has been a miscopying.

44. *Beijū*, musicians who accompanied the festival dancers. Who the relatives in question (the text actually says only "ones whom I would be thinking of") might be, we are not told.

45. A temple east of the old city and within the present city.

46. Which means "China." What it refers to here has not been determined. Perhaps the messenger means only to suggest that the fire is a great distance away.

47. There were taboos that lasted for a year and were in addition to daily taboos. See Introduction, pages 17-18.

48. Wooden or paper tabs posted about the person of one in-volved in *monoimi*.

49. An obscure sentence. The concluding clause reads *taoruru kata ni tachikaeru*, which may mean the same thing as the clause quoted in Note 27, Book 1.

50. Fujiwara Koretada, Kaneie's brother, became Regent in 970 and Great Minister of State in 971.

51. A short distance north of the old palace, not far from the present Daitokuji. This is possibly the return procession from the festival.

52. To be distinguished by the sleeves trailing from under the blinds (see illustration: Appendix, Plate 6). It appears to be sleeves that captivate Michitsuna.

53. The usual pun: *aoi*, "hollyhock" and "meeting day." "Now that the hollyhocks are past, when is the next meeting day to be?"

54. *Kokinshū* No. 982, author unknown: "My hut is at the foot of Mt. Miwa. Let him who will come calling—he will know it by the cedar-lined gate." Mt. Miwa, in Yamato, is brought in because the lady is from that province.

55. The reference is to the story of Tamayori-hime in the *Kojiki*. Tamayori-hime, who lived at Miwa, became pregnant by a handsome gentleman who visited her every night but whom she was unable to identify to her surprised parents. At their sug-gestion she attached a thread to his cloak one evening, and the following morning it was found to leave through a keyhole and

lead to a shrine. Hence it was evident that Tamayori-hime's friend was a god.

56. Possibly because in the Month of the *Unohana* (a white-flowering shrub), the Fourth Month, there are no *unohana* this year. The intercalary month has pushed the seasons askew.

57. Offerings, once offered, could be consumed. This seems to be such a "taken-down" offering.

58. Which were pulled for the *Tango no Sekku,* the Fifth of the Fifth Month.

59. *Kusudama,* "medicine balls," cloth or net bags filled with herbs and decorated with flowers and streamers, were made on the *Tango no Sekku.* It has been suggested that the process described here in such vague terms may somehow be related to them.

60. Probably Senshi (Akiko), Tokihime's daughter.

61. Sone Yoshitada, a talented and rather pathetic figure, composed this poem after he had been evicted from a poetry meet to which he had gone uninvited: "One would not mind waiting if the night wind were not so cold."

62. East of the Kamo Shrine, and northeast of the city.

63. *Nawazemi,* a large cicada.

64. *Shika, shika,* in imitation of the cicada.

65. *Soba* or *nishikigi.* A shrub, genus *Evonymus.*

66. One of several possible interpretations, none of which seems entirely satisfactory.

67. "He came to have no house," the text says. Perhaps he had to move to avoid some transgression or other. See Introduction, page 18.

68. *Madokoro* or *mandokoro,* the business office of a high-ranking nobleman.

69. *Tsukutsukubōshi* or *kutsukutsubōshi,* a cicada heard in late summer and autumn and named in imitation of its hum.

70. From the *Utsubo Monogatari.*

71. In the Eighth Month? The wrestling tournament was customarily held in the Seventh Month, and the *kaeri aruji,* "return banquet," concluded the festivities. There is no record in the histories, however, of a tournament for this year, and both here and in the reference three paragraphs later, *kaeri aruji* is an arbitrary reworking of what has been taken for a garble. Whether this is in fact the annual court tournament is therefore not certain.

72. The text becomes difficult to follow, and perhaps a passage is missing here. It is odd that both here and at the point on page 148 where the text appears to break off the author is on the verge of describing a dream. If the succeeding passages can be interpreted as descriptions of the dreams in question, then

perhaps the text is complete as it stands; such an interpretation, however, does not seem to hold very well in either
case.

73. The swan's tracks indicate also the letter written with that
pointed object. Shirahama, "White Beach," said once to have
been a place name in the province of Tajima, is introduced to
prepare the way for the snow.

74. Or the Isonokami Jingū in Yamato. It is a favorite with poets
because *furu* indicates the passage of time.

75. Another Yamato place name, and another favorite with the
poets. The One-Word God, Hitokotonushi-no-kami, lived
there.

76. An import from China. Dokujin, God of the Hearth (more
accurately, perhaps, "of the Real Estate"), moved about the
premises season by season. If it became necessary to repair the
apartments in which he was currently resident, the owner of
the establishment had to move out by way of reparation.

77. Koretada, Kaneie's brother. His death touched off a family
feud. See Introduction, pages 15–16.

78. In fact, he was not doing so well. See Introduction, page 16.

79. An obscure sentence.

80. *Katamon,* a tight weave in which the pattern sinks into the
background. Patterns were woven into the cloth, not printed.
Aya, used here to describe Kaneie's outer robe, indicates any
weave with a pattern.

81. *Kokin Rokujō:* "My thoughts have not been quenched by this
long rain. On the contrary, they seem to be putting out new
shoots."

82. See page 132.

83. At Nara. The Fujiwara family shrine.

84. The residence of the ex-Emperor Reizei.

85. *Kandachime,* third rank and above and Councilors (*Sangi*)
fourth rank and above. As with the previous archery meet,
(pages 80–81), it is difficult to see what goes on here. The
passage seems to contain a number of technical terms.

86. For the Iwashimizu Hachiman Shrine, southwest of Kyoto.
The interim festival (*rinjisai*) was held in the Third Month.

87. This fire is reported in the *Nihon Giryaku.* It destroyed more
than three hundred houses and seems to have resulted from
arson.

88. Onakatomi Yoshinobu, *Shikashū* No. 224 and *Kokin Rokujō:*
"My thoughts are like the watch fires; quiet during the day,
they blaze up every night."

89. The Iris Festival, *Tango no Sekku,* the Fifth of the Fifth Month.

90. The poem is an obscure one. Perhaps Michitsuna and his
mother do not understand it.

91. *Ebukuro*. Apparently a sort of wicker basket or bag with a cloth pouch inside it.

92. The usual pun on *kochi*, "east wind" and "this way."

93. The text says only "the person I relied on."

94. Hirohata Nakagawa, on the eastern outskirts of the city. The Nakagawa served as the city moat.

95. The text is garbled. According to one theory, she is here rejoicing in the abundance of water. Cf. Note 96.

96. "Both on the inside and on the outside," the text says. This could refer to two rivers, possibly the main Nakagawa and a branch that was diverted to run through the garden. For an example of such a diversion of the Nakagawa see "Hahakigi" ("The Broom Tree") in the *Genji Monogatari*.

97. I.e., she had hoped Kaneie would continue to come in spite of her move. There is a pun on *toko*, "bed" and "river bed."

98. New rice was roasted, hulls and all.

99. "Am I to go on with this unrewarding correspondence all my life?"

100. Possibly the wife of Sugawara Takasue and the mother of the author of the *Sarashina Nikki*. The year of her birth is not known, but she must have been some thirty or forty years younger than Michitsuna's mother. The tardiness of the author's congratulations here may indicate resentment at her father's continued philandering.

101. *Tachihaki no Osa*. Why he should be entrusted with the mission is not clear, unless perhaps he is a relative.

102. Apparently both apology for the long delay and congratulation for the child.

103. The time sequence here is complicated. The robe is sent to Kaneie on New Year's Day; there follows a flashback to the Eleventh Month and the birth of Tomoyasu's child; then, with the plums and all, we are again in the First Month; the two pilgrimages apparently take place in the First Month; and then suddenly we are back again in the Tenth Month. A most confusing use of flashbacks; or possibly the text is mutilated.

104. *Nabi*, which is written with the characters for "devil-chasing fire." It is not known, however, what observance is indicated. From the Kamakura period ritual fires were lighted in the palace on the night of the Fifteenth of the First Month, but there is no record of such a ceremony during the Heian period.

105. Fujiwara Asatada, *Gosenshū* No. 70: "The flowers are in bloom, but I want only to leave this torment for a mountain temple."

106. *Kiokonai*, the meaning of which is unclear. It might be that Michitsuna conducts religious services to help himself get a position.

107. *Uma no Suke,* second in command of one of two offices charged with managing the imperial stables.

108. Probably Kaneie's younger brother Tōnori. Whoever he is, he dominates much of the rest of the diary. The reader should not be surprised at his subsequent suit for the hand of the author's adopted daughter, who is his own niece. Such things happened in the Heian period.

109. The text becomes incoherent here, and possibly something is missing. See Note 72, above.

110. This phrase refers to a passage in the *Yamato Monogatari* : "It was at Yogawa—not particularly deep in the mountain, but still Hiei lay back toward the city." Yogawa is to the north of the main temples on Mt. Hiei.

111. Possibly a quotation.

112. The text is garbled here.

113. As on the trip to Ishiyama, the author seems to be on foot.

114. Two interpretations seem possible : Michitsuna rests somewhere before coming in to see the author ; or she is already in bed when he arrives. The latter seems to strain the text a bit. It is also possible that the text is garbled.

115. Musashi is probably in attendance on the author or the child and is to be used by the Kami as a pretext for visiting the author's house. It appears to have been not uncommon for a gentleman to approach a lady's lady preparatory to approaching the lady herself.

116. A devious pun. The Isonokami Jingū was at Furu in Yamato. *Furu* means "to rain." Hence Isonokami comes to stand for rain.

117. A not too unlikely interpretation of a most obscure sentence.

118. *Nōshi.* See illustration: Appendix, Plate 4.

119. *Ei,* a stiff netting attached to the back of the cap.

120. Presumably it was in an outbuilding that the shutters were up and the author's women were caught in that embarrassing position.

121. *Warōda,* a round straw mat woven of straw or rushes.

122. In the *hisashi,* between the veranda and the main part of the room.

123. *Shaku,* a thin piece of wood about a foot long and three inches wide, tapering gently toward the lower end. It seems to have originally served as a sort of prompter, carrying instructions for ceremonial occasions, but gradually it came to be an indication of rank. The Kami seems here to be most carefully dressed.

124. There is a textual obscurity here. One view has it that the rain has stopped.

125. As becomes clear slightly later, Michitsuna is scheduled to participate in the Kamo Festival in the Fourth Month.

126. Or perhaps: " 'There is nothing to be upset about,' he answered." The crucial word in the sentence could be either positive or negative.

127. Of the vestal for the Kamo Festival. The dead dog of course defiles Michitsuna and disqualifies him for the event.

128. A possible alternative explanation would be that he presses Michitsuna to take up his case with the author.

129. A pun on *aoi* "hollyhock" and "day of meeting." The hollyhock was the symbol of the Kamo Festival in the Fourth Month.

130. This sentence is unclear unless it may be assumed that he has open designs on the author herself.

131. Actually a *sudare,* a reed or bamboo blind.

132. Literally, "the calendar is almost unrolled." A proverb?

133. The abdicated Emperor, Reizei.

134. Unfortunately this crucial sentence is garbled. Another possible reconstruction has him moving not forward but backward, out to the corridor.

135. When?

136. *Onna e,* literally "women pictures." *Onna e* seem to have been colored pictures in contrast to *otoko e,* ink washes.

137. One of the pavilions terminating the two forward corridors in standard *shinden* architecture.

138. Based on one of the most famous poems, No. 1093, in the *Kokinshū* ("If I am unfaithful to you, that day the waves will break over Sue no Matsuyama"—it has appeared earlier in this diary), waves have come to stand for a faithless lover.

139. *Kokinshū* No. 992, author unknown: "The grass under the grove of Oaraki is withered. No pony relishes it, no harvester gathers it."

140. Unclear. Possibly a quotation.

141. Feelings about the cuckoo were oddly mixed. It was listened for eagerly, but at the same time it was associated with the dead and inspired certain forebodings. An overabundance of cuckoos seems to have been a bad omen.

142. *Muma-bune.* The following exchange has to do with the Kami's desire for an early end to the courtship.

143. Or the people at the author's house. The designation is vague.

144. *Kataori,* a fine, close weave.

145. The Fifth of the Fifth Month.

146. Iris roots and leaves were laid on the roof for the Iris Festival.

147. *Kusudama.* See Note 59 above.

148. More unhappiness about the cuckoo. See Note 141 above.

149. The Emperor Daigo in the *Shūishū* No. 111 and *Kokin Rokujō:* "The mountain cuckoo sings here on the day of the iris root." Rather commonplace in translation, the poem contains a pun which turns it into a love song.

150. It is clear that he read it, but it is not clear whether he admits having done so.

151. *Kokinshū* No. 720, author unknown: "And is one to take it seriously when the River Asuka, which has flowed so steadily, dams up for a time?"

152. There is a "pivot word" here: *u,* joining *mi no u,* "one's melancholy," and *unohana,* a white-flowering shrub.

153. This is a guess. It is not clear how much she inks out.

154. *Sakyō no Kami.* The government of Kyoto was divided into two sections, the Left or East (of the axial Suzaku Avenue) and the Right or West. This is Fujiwara Tōmoto, Kaneie's brother.

155. It is not likely that the court would go into mourning for such a minor figure as Tōmoto. Possibly this is the beginning of the smallpox epidemic described later, and the court is in a sort of prophylactic retreat.

156. *Azarikareba,* meaning obscure.

157. Both letters are obscure, and the texts are mutilated.

158. "The big river." Probably the Kamogawa.

159. Fujiwara Takakata and Yoshitaka, sons of Koretada and nephews of Kaneie.

160. If it is still she. It is now two and a half years since Michitsuna's first letter.

161. *Jūten.* Underlinings perhaps.

162. Suishi (Yasuko), whose mother was the daughter of Kuniaki (the Omi of this diary?), was born in 974.

163. A thick white or grayish paper, sometimes with a furrowed surface. It was originally produced in Michinoku, the province of Mutsu, in northern Japan.

164. See pages 159 and 162.

165. Kaneie's brother Kanemichi, with whom Kaneie is currently feuding. The significance of this episode is not clear, but it would appear that Tōnori, out of resentment against Kaneie, has shown the author's letter to Kanemichi.

166. *Kamo Rinjisai,* in the Eleventh Month.

167. Or possibly the author wept as she saw Michitsuna leave.

168. *Birōge,* a carriage with sides of woven palm fronds.

169. "Red people and black people." The fifth rank wore red robes on formal occasions, the fourth rank and above black.

170. Or during the procession. The "high-ranking carriages" are apparently spectators, but the time sequence is obscure.

171. "The *yamabuki.*" Apparently low-grade officials were so designated because of the flowers (the *yamabuki* is a yellow

flower related to the rose) they wore in their caps on the day of the festival.

172. Or it brought a moment of satisfaction to the author? This sentence is grammatically confused.

173. "She seemed to be from the vicinity of Yatsuhashi." Yatsuhashi is a place name in the province of Mikawa. Hence she is the daughter of the Governor of Mikawa? Another theory has it that she is from a Yatsuhashi ("Eight Bridges") in Kyoto, the location of which, however, has not been established.

174. The One-Word God. (See Note 75 above.) There also seems to have been a One-Word God in the vicinity of Kyoto, a fact which argues in favor of the Kyoto Yatsuhashi.

175. An involved poem built around the place-name Yatsuhashi and its many-branched river (*kumode*), which the author (or Michitsuna if the poem is his) uses to suggest a multiplicity of directions. There is a pun on *fumi*, "tracks" and "handwriting" or "letter."

176. The pun on *fumi* repeated: "I need only follow up my letters." The *Zokugosenshū* credits this poem to Kaneie.

177. The *kumo*, "spider," of *kumode*, "spider legs" or "many branches" (see Michitsuna's second poem), now is incorporated into *kumoji*, "cloudy way."

178. "Cloudy way" is also "spider's way," bringing the metaphor back to the eight bridges of Yatsuhashi. The spider stands also for a visiting lover.

179. The pun is repeated.

180. The image of the clouds is used to introduce the crane, which uses successfully enough the bridge the lady so underestimates.

181. *Sobaminuru* contains a pun on *sobamu*, "to incline in one direction" or "to go askew," and *sobamiru*, "to see a *soba*." The lady's "I have seen" comes attached to a branch of *soba*, "brocade tree."

182. The usual pun on *matsu*, "wait" and "pine," indicates that the lady does not intend to give in easily. The exchange between Michitsuna and the lady from Mikawa seems to break off here. Although the author nowhere indicates that such is the case, the rest of the poems are best understood as passing between her and Kaneie. This final section of the diary has a fragmentary air about it, as though it were made up of random notes never beaten into shape. The author's motive in suddenly beginning correspondence with Kaneie again, if indeed she does, is not explained.

183. There was an intercalary Tenth Month in 974, which would make New Year's Day, 975, as late as it ever came under the

Japanese lunar calendar. Hence *Setsubun*, midway between the winter solstice and the vernal equinox, falls in the old year.

184. The metaphor of the waves (see Note 138, above) is given a somewhat unusual turn.

185. The author seems to be making fun of Kaneie's irascibleness.

186. A "pivot word" here joins the author's laments to the bare branch.

187. The Seventh of the First Month.

188. It is not clear to what ritual this refers.

189. The text breaks off in the middle of a sentence. "The Collected Poems of the Mother of Michitsuna" are usually printed at the end of the journal. They were edited by someone other than the author, and are of little interest even to the specialist. Those who wish to examine them will find them appended to the first version of this translation (*Transactions of the Asiatic Society of Japan*, Third Series, Vol. 4, Tokyo, June, 1955).

Appendix

The Heian Setting: Illustrations and Map

1. The *shinden*-style Heian mansion
2. Panoramic view of the Heian garden
3. The Heian garden viewed from inside a mansion
4. Heian courtiers in formal and informal dress
5. Gentlemen attired in *kariginu*
6. Scenes from the Hollyhock Festival
7. Detail from the "Ishiyama-dera Engi Emaki"
8. Map of the Kyoto-Osaka region

Plate 1 : This reconstruction by Mr. Mori Osamu of a typical Heian-period mansion shows the (1) *moya*, (2) *nishi no tai*, (3) *higashi no tai*, (4) *watari-dono*, and (5) inner gate. The position of the *tsuri-dono* and *izumi-dono* (6 and 7), here hidden in the clouds, can be seen from the garden in Plate 2. The passages behind the main buildings lead to one or more rows of similar buildings.

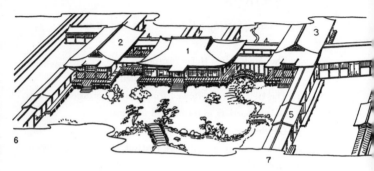

Plate 2 : The Heian garden as reconstructed by Mr. Mori Osamu from that of the Higashi Sonjo-in, which seems not to have had the customary out-building to the east.

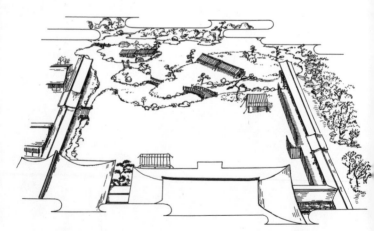

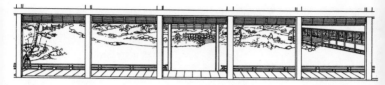

Plate 3: The Heian garden of Plate 2 as Mr. Mori Osamu imagines it to have appeared from inside the *moya*, or "mother chamber," of the main unit of a mansion as described in the Introduction (pages 20-21).

Plate 4: Informal gentleman, wearing *nōshi*, and formal ladies with *mo* and *karaginu* (see page 22). As the scene is from the Kamakura-period scroll "Kasuga Gongen Emaki," the architecture and furnishings cannot be considered accurate for the Heian period.

Plate 5: Gentlemen in *kariginu*, as worn by the Prince on page 68. The tearful scene is a detail from the "Ban Dainagon Emaki."

Plate 6: The Hollyhock Festival in three scenes of the "Nenjū Gyōji Emaki." The lady's sleeves hanging from the carriage in the upper left of the bottom panel possibly are like those with which Michitsuna, on page 136, fell in love.

Plate 7: Detail from the "Ishiyama-dera Engi Emaki" showing representation of the dream of the author, described on page 90. She had this dream during her first night in the Ishiyama-dera on the pilgrimage she took in the Seventh Month of 970. The scroll, a work of the late Kamakura or early Muromachi period, is the property of the Ishiyama-dera.

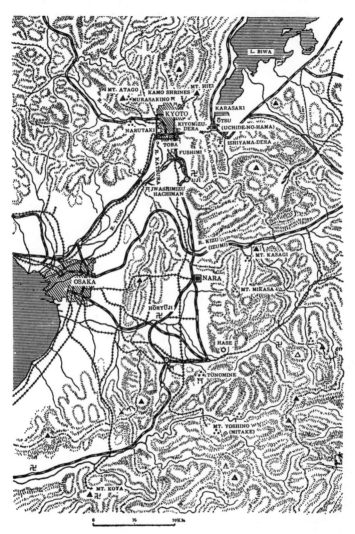

Plate 8: Map of the Kyoto-Osaka region showing the principal places mentioned in the text. The modern railway network is included to guide the reader who knows the area. The author's routes south and east from Kyoto generally followed the present private railways, represented by the narrower lines. The rectangle imposed on the site of modern Kyoto marks the limits of the Heian city.

Other TUT BOOKS available:

BACHELOR'S HAWAII *by Boye de Mente*

BACHELOR'S JAPAN *by Boye de Mente*

BACHELOR'S MEXICO *by Boye de Mente*

A BOOK OF NEW ENGLAND LEGENDS AND FOLK LORE *by Samuel Adams Drake*

THE BUDDHA TREE *by Fumio Niwa; translated by Kenneth Strong*

CALABASHES AND KINGS: An Introduction to Hawaii *by Stanley D. Porteus*

CHINA COLLECTING IN AMERICA *by Alice Morse Earle*

CHINESE COOKING MADE EASY *by Rosy Tseng*

CHOI OI!: The Lighter Side of Vietnam *by Tony Zidek*

THE COUNTERFEITER and Other Stories *by Yasushi Inoue; translated by Leon Picon*

CURIOUS PUNISHMENTS OF BYGONE DAYS *by Alice Morse Earle*

CUSTOMS AND FASHIONS IN OLD NEW ENGLAND *by Alice Morse Earle*

DINING IN SPAIN *by Gerrie Beene and Lourdes Miranda King*

EXOTICS AND RETROSPECTIVES *by Lafcadio Hearn*

FIRST YOU TAKE A LEEK: A Guide to Elegant Eating Spiced with Culinary Capers *by Maxine J. Saltonstall*

FIVE WOMEN WHO LOVED LOVE *by Saikaku Ihara; translated by William Theodore de Bary*

A FLOWER DOES NOT TALK: Zen Essays *by Abbot Zenkei Shibayama of the Nanzenji*

FOLK LEGENDS OF JAPAN *by Richard M. Dorson*

GLEANINGS IN BUDDHA-FIELDS: Studies of Hand and Soul in the Far East *by Lafcadio Hearn*

GOING NATIVE IN HAWAII: A Poor Man's Guide to Paradise *by Timothy Head*

HAIKU IN ENGLISH *by Harold G. Henderson*

HARP OF BURMA *by Michio Takeyama; translated by Howard Hibbett*

HAWAII: End of the Rainbow *by Kazuo Miyamoto*

THE HAWAIIAN GUIDE BOOK for Travelers *by Henry M. Whitney*

HAWAIIAN PHRASE BOOK

HISTORIC MANSIONS AND HIGHWAYS AROUND BOSTON *by Samuel Adams Drake*

HISTORICAL AND GEOGRAPHICAL DICTIONARY OF JAPAN *by E. Papinot*

A HISTORY OF JAPANESE LITERATURE *by W. G. Aston*

HOMEMADE ICE CREAM AND SHERBERT *by Sheila MacNiven Cameron*

HOW TO READ CHARACTER: A New Illustrated Handbook of Phrenology and Physiognomy, for Students and Examiners *by Samuel R. Wells*

IN GHOSTLY JAPAN *by Lafcadio Hearn*

INDIAN RIBALDRY *by Randor Guy*

JAPAN: An Attempt at Interpretation *by Lafcadio Hearn*

THE JAPANESE ABACUS *by Takashi Kojima*

THE JAPANESE ARE LIKE THAT *by Ichiro Kawasaki*

JAPANESE ETIQUETTE: An Introduction *by the World Fellowship Committee of the Tokyo Y.W.C.A.*

THE JAPANESE FAIRY BOOK *compiled by Yei Theodora Ozaki*

JAPANESE FOLK-PLAYS: The Ink-Smeared Lady and Other Kyogen *translated by Shio Sakanishi*

JAPANESE FOOD AND COOKING *by Stuart Griffin*

JAPANESE HOMES AND THIER SURROUNDINGS *by Edward S. Morse*

A JAPANESE MISCELLANY *by Lafcadio Hearn*

JAPANESE RECIPES *by Tatsuji Tada*

JAPANESE TALES OF MYSTERY & IMAGINATION *by Edogawa Rampo; translated by James B. Harris*

JAPANESE THINGS: Being Notes on Various Subjects Connected with Japan *by Basil Hall Chamberlain*

THE JOKE'S ON JUDO *by Donn Draeger and Ken Tremayne*

THE KABUKI HANDBOOK *by Aubrey S. Halford and Giovanna M. Halford*

KAPPA *by Ryūnosuke Akutagawa; translated by Geoffrey Bownas*

KOKORO: Hints and Echoes of Japanese Inner Life *by Lafcadio Hearn*

KOREAN FOLK TALES *by Im Bang and Yi Ryuk; translated by James S. Gale*

KOTTŌ: Being Japanese Curios, with Sundry Cobwebs *by Lafcadio Hearn*

KWAIDAN: Stories and Studies of Strange Things *by Lafcadio Hearn*

LET'S STUDY JAPANESE *by Jun Maeda*

THE LIFE OF BUDDHA *by A. Ferdinand Herold*

MODERN JAPANESE PRINTS: A Contemporary Selection *edited by Yuji Abe*

NIHONGI: Chronicles of Japan from the Earliest Times to A.D. 697 *by W. G. Aston*

OLD LANDMARKS AND HISTORIC PERSONAGES OF BOSTON *by Samuel Adams Drake*

ORIENTAL FORTUNE TELLING *by Jimmei Shimano; translated by Togo Taguchi*

PHYSICAL FITNESS: A Practical Program *by Clark Hatch*

READ JAPANESE TODAY *by Len Walsh*

SELF DEFENSE SIMPLIFIED IN PICTURES *by Don Hepler*

SHADOWINGS *by Lafcadio Hearn*

A SHORT SYNOPSIS OF THE MOST ESSENTIAL POINTS IN HAWAIIAN GRAMMAR *by W. D. Alexander*

THE STORY BAG: A Collection of Korean Folk Tales *by Kim So-un; translated by Setsu Higashi*

SUMI-E: An Introduction to Ink Painting *by Nanae Momiyama*

SUN-DIALS AND ROSES OF YESTERDAY *by Alice Morse Earle*

THE TEN FOOT SQUARE HUT AND TALES OF THE HEIKE: Being Two Thirteenth-century Japanese classics, the "Hojoki" and selections from the "Heike Monogatari" *translated by A. L. Sadler*

THIS SCORCHING EARTH *by Donald Richie*

TIMES-SQUARE SAMURAI or the Improbable Japanese Occupation of New York *by Robert B. Johnson and Billie Niles Chadbourne*

TO LIVE IN JAPAN *by Mary Lee O'Neal and Virginia Woodruff*

THE TOURIST AND THE REAL JAPAN *by Boye de Mente*

TOURS OF OKINAWA: A Souvenir Guide to Places of Interest *compiled by Gasei Higa, Isamu Fuchaku, and Zenkichi Toyama*

TWO CENTURIES OF COSTUME IN AMERICA *by Alice Morse Earle*

TYPHOON! TYPHOON! An Illustrated Haiku Sequence *by Lucile M. Bogue*

UNBEATEN TRACKS IN JAPAN: An Account of Travels in the Interior Including Visits to the Aborigines of Yezo and the Shrine of Nikko *by Isabella L. Bird*

ZILCH! The Marine Corps' Most Guarded Secret *by Roy Delgado*

Please order from your bookstore or write directly to:

CHARLES E. TUTTLE CO., INC.
Suido 1-chome, 2–6, Bunkyo-ku, Tokyo 112

or:

CHARLES E. TUTTLE CO., INC.
Rutland, Vermont 05701 U.S.A.